Fela's Story: Memoir of a Displaced Family

Fela's Story
Memoir of a Displaced Family

Phyllis Beren

International Psychoanalytic Books (IPBooks)
New York • http://www.IPBooks.net

A Note from the Author about the Cover Picture:
The cover tempera drawing is of my maternal grandparents home in Russia and the couple in front are my grandparents. Their neighbor, Senya Gorodetsky, an artist, had signed his name at the bottom with two dates. He drew the house as it was in 1931, and when he came to America in 1980 he made a copy for me. That is why there are two dates under his name.

Published by IPBooks, Queens, NY
Online at: www.IPBooks.net

Copyright © 2019 Phyllis Beren

All rights reserved. No part of this book may be used or reproduced in any manner whatsoever including Internet usage, without written permission of the author.

Cover Design by Kathy Kovacic, Blackthorn Studio
Back Cover photo by Joyce Grossbard

Typesetting and formatting services by Self-Publishing Lab

ISBN: 978-1-949093-42-1

In memory of my parents Sonja and Rachmil

Contents

Introduction	1
1. Waiting	7
2. Elizabeth's Story	15
3. My Mother's Story	49
4. Behind the Iron Curtain	65
5. In Limbo: Ulm	99
6. Föhrenwald DP Camp	115
7. California Strasse 21	139
Epilogue: Fela's Story	161
Acknowledgements	173
References	179

Introduction

In the last years of her life, I noticed two significant alterations in my mother: her increased preoccupation with her Holocaust past and changes in her memory. It took me years to accept the change that took place in her memory because I had always been in awe of her astounding capacity for recall. When I was two years old she recited endless Russian poetry and nursery rhymes, and when I was an adult, she would recite these same poems and ask if I remembered them. She helped me with my algebra when I was in high school, performing complicated mathematical calculations in her head. The decline of her sharp memory, at first barely perceptible, slowly picked up speed and ultimately became the progression of Alzheimer's.

Unlike her stock of retained knowledge, when it came to answering questions about our life during and after the war, she offered a confused narrative. Only when she was much older, but prior to her loss of memory, did she change her attitude about the past and develop a growing interest in learning more about the Holocaust. She would speak to me about books and articles she read, films she watched, and stories she heard. When this kind of remembrance began to occur, I experienced an uneasy feeling, as if my mother were illegitimately identifying herself as a Holocaust survivor. I say illegitimately because as I was growing up she had set herself apart from my father and his extended family. My father's family felt connected to their past and spoke of family and friends lost in the Holocaust. Gradually, I came to understand that she was identifying and recognizing her own story in what others had remembered, experienced, and written about the war years, specifically about the Holocaust. As she shared her newly awakened discoveries with me, she frequently followed up by saying, "Phyllis, you know, that's what *we* went through."

As an only child born in Russia close to the end of the war, arriving in the United States at the age of nearly nine from a Displaced Persons Camp in Germany, I was caught between my mother's desire not to look back, to begin a fresh life, and my father's reticence towards his new country, his mourning of what had been lost. The contrast between my mother and father was glaring, and it left me not knowing where to place myself. Ultimately, like many children, it became more natural to adopt my mother's view and embrace becoming an assimilated American. America was a country that had a name. In the past, I did not even have the name of a country I could call my own.

For many years I had contemplated writing a memoir about my experience of assimilation. The memoir was to be about a young girl who arrived in America in 1952 from a displaced persons camp in Germany, settled in Chicago, and entered first grade at the age of nine speaking not a word of English. She now lived with her parents in an apartment, no longer sharing her living quarters with her extended family or with strangers. The memoir was to cover the years from grade school through college. It would have as its focus the place of family and friendships in her life, including the sweeping changes that took place in America during the sixties and the influence of those changes on her late adolescence and young womanhood. For many years, I thought on and off about writing this memoir, even going so far as looking into memoir writing workshops. But something always seemed to stop me from fully committing to this endeavor.

My desire to write the present memoir was different. I experienced an urgency to undertake this task due to the changes in my mother. And as readiness is all, I serendipitously came upon the perfect writing group. But I still did not know what I would write about.

For years my mother and I spoke on the phone at least once a week. Her husband, my stepfather Chuck, had now been dead for over fifteen years and my mother was still working and living alone in her home in Skokie, Illinois, a northern suburb of Chicago.

I began to sense that something was different about her, but if asked what I meant I would not have been able to put my finger on it. It was not just her new interest in reading books about the Holocaust and her awakened curiosity about her past; there was also something different in her tone of voice. It was unfamiliar, more detached, distant, as if she were in her own world. My mother, who was an opinionated, strong-willed and quite inflexible person, could also show another side. In a more relaxed state of mind she could be spontaneous, adaptable, and willing to accommodate another person's wishes. But her spontaneous and adaptable side seemed to diminish in her late seventies as she became increasingly inflexible, wedded to her routines. She would get up at an ungodly hour to dress and drive to the station where she'd park her car and take a commuter train to her office in downtown Chicago. After returning in the evening, she'd prepare dinner for herself, do her bookkeeping, and then settle in with her cat to watch television or read. She saw fewer friends and seemed content to busy herself at home. She was not, as she had been earlier, insistent that I visit her often; instead she increasingly found excuses as to why she could not visit me in New York.

This was particularly striking since she really enjoyed the city, but now she preferred to stay put at home with her cat. When we spoke on the phone she asked about what was going on in my life, but she delivered her questions in a mechanical tone that conveyed little affect. After our conversation ended I felt an uneasiness come over me, perhaps caused by her tone and emotional withdrawal. At first, I experienced a sense of relief from the frequent guilt she induced in me for not visiting or calling more often; yet over time, as her detachment persisted, I also felt a growing sadness and sense of loss. I became aware that she was repeating herself, not remembering what I had already told her the last time we spoke. Her answers to my questions were vague or abrupt, as if she did not want to go into any details.

One year my mother, who never forgot my birthday, didn't call. I felt perplexed and wondered, "Is she angry with me?" A couple of days passed and still no call. I did not know what to do. Should I call her and demand to know why she had forgotten my birthday? Would I make her feel bad that she had forgotten? Did I want to make her feel bad for forgetting? When I subsequently spoke with her and she asked me what I had been doing, I mentioned that my husband had taken me out to dinner on my birthday. She fell silent and then said something that made me realize she sounded very confused. I felt terrible for reminding her of my birthday and causing her distress.

Her loss of memory, increasing over a number of years, rapidly gathered speed. I became aware of a parallel process occurring in me. The changes I perceived in her mood and in her thinking left me disorientated and confused. I felt her drifting away, and then came the day when I could no longer deny that my mother was suffering from dementia. With this dawning realization, I had to face the fact that one day my mother would no longer know me as her daughter. I suspect it was on that day that I began to feel an urgency to fill the gaps in my family's history, including revisiting our intense and complicated relationship.

I often felt myself to be the parentified child, responsible for taking care of her. Perhaps as the caretaker, this renewed desire to write a memoir was an extension of my lifelong feeling of responsibility. Now the weight of her real-life situation made taking care of her a necessity. For all these reasons, it seemed quite natural that I should take on the task of holding my mother's memories just as they were slipping away from her. Writing about our lives was also a way of holding on to her, a way to stitch together my own fragmented history and to recall my own lost memories. To write this memoir I needed to learn more about my mother, my father, their marriage, my extended family, and their journey from Europe to America.

Introduction

In August of 2007 at the age of eighty-five, my mother had to leave the house she had lived in for the past forty-five years and enter a nursing home. The move was long overdue but she had fought it fiercely, until a broken hip and a difficult recuperation made it clear that she could no longer live on her own. This move opened an opportunity to revisit my unanswered questions about the past, a past that had puzzled and confused me most of my life. Paradoxically, the remembrance and recovery of my family's history began to take shape on the floor of a nursing home devoted to Alzheimer's patients.

The floor designated for Alzheimer's patients turned out to be surprisingly pleasant, not as grim as I had anticipated. My mother had a private room, as did all the residents in this home. The staff was helpful and caring, and my mother's private care person, Maria, was a warm Mexican woman with four children of her own. She was totally devoted to my mother, and my mother, who could be very critical and not allow new people into her life, allowed Maria into hers. They were good for one another, and Maria says it was my mother's influence that made her decide to continue her education and become a certified caretaker. Among the residents on the floor were a number of Holocaust survivors as well as Russian Jews who left Russia after Perestroika.

Having now placed my mother safely in the residence, I had the task of going through the contents of the house she and my stepfather bought when they married in 1966. Standing in her home, fragments of images and memories from the past flooded my mind as I looked at the old fixtures, worn furniture, my stepfather's drawings on the walls and framed photos of me at every stage of my life.

What I saw was a home frozen in time. I finally forced myself to look into the drawers that contained brittle and yellowing documents brought from Germany, the documents I had long avoided reading. An old issue surfaced: did I or did I not want to know? I never understood why I had such difficulty studying history in high school and college. It was as if a fog seemed to envelop me. While standing in my mother's home, I suddenly understood that I was ambivalent about fully knowing my own history. It was as if my mother's failing memory had lifted the fog and hastened my wish to see and to know.

I am in the fortunate position of having a number of close relatives and friends who live in Chicago, in particular my cousin Elizabeth who knows me from birth. They were also very close to my mother and would make themselves available on the weekends when I travelled to Chicago alone or with my husband to visit my mother in the residence. My friends and relatives have always played a significant role in my life, as well as in the lives of my parents. They have come to represent a continuity of place and time. In many gatherings at their homes and in the residence with my mother, we could share stories and memories of the past.

In writing this memoir, I have often felt as if I had fallen down a hole like Alice in Wonderland, surrounded by strange yet familiar figures speaking different languages, some of which I understood, others needing a dictionary to translate. Just as I moved from country to country and from place to place, so I traded in languages: Russian to Yiddish and Polish, then to German and finally English. I carry the remnants of all of these languages in my mind and at different times and places echoes of them return. I keep coming back to the place memory has in one's life. Early memories clamor for recognition, for permission to exist, to be illuminated, to bridge the gap between past and present in the hope that our lives will gain a greater continuity. But simply recapturing memories is often not sufficient to offer continuity. Writing this memoir helped in the process. It forced a reexamination and reconsideration of the past, offering more shape and coherence to my ruptured history.

And so what follows is a memoir that begins in my mother's nursing home where I found myself eerily back in Europe, surrounded by people speaking to me in Yiddish, Polish, and Russian—the languages of my history.

CHAPTER 1

Waiting

"Will they put us someplace? Will you go ask the lady when can we go?"

I am trying to follow my mother's disjointed train of thought. "Where are we going?" I ask.

Looking out the window, my mother stands, points her finger, struggling to find words.

"Little houses, see. Over there, we have to go."

Where is she right now? Where does she think we need to go? All I can see out the window are tall buildings peering through the trees. Currently, in her mind's eye, she is not in her room on the fifth floor of the Alzheimer's residence located just a few miles from her former home of more than forty years.

Again she repeats, "We have to go," still gazing out the window, seeing the reflection of the scene in her mind.

Visualizing a small village in Russia, I imagine what she might be seeing. My image comes from a tempera drawing, hanging in my New York City apartment, a gift to my mother from Senya, a family friend, neighbor, and artist who emigrated from the Soviet Union to this country in 1980. The drawing is signed and dated 1981, and below the signature is written: Gomel 1932. It is a piece of folk art showing the home where my mother grew up. The house with its rustic windows, sloping roof and small chimney is drawn in simple lines creating a cluster of triangular and rectangular shapes. It is surrounded by similar houses, creating a storybook scene. A fenced-in vegetable garden sits on one side of the house next to a structure that could be a shed. On the opposite side of the house is a tall wooden fence with a door leading to the entrance. The painting draws your eyes to a clothesline; linen hangs blowing in the wind. On small stools in front of their home, my grandparents sit. They look young and relaxed, my grandmother in a plain white summer dress, her long black hair tied behind her neck, my grandfather beside her, legs crossed, in a blue shirt. They seem engaged in conversation. My mother would have been ten years old had she been present in this scene.

Small villages in Russia? Has she returned to her home in Gomel? Is she back in the war having to flee her home? Or is she leaving Russia for Poland?

"Are we in Russia now?" I ask.

"Not exactly Russia," she replies, once more pointing towards some imagined place from a distant past.

She speaks in halting phrases, saying the words 'border,' 'towns,' 'papers.' Are we once more crossing borders? Or is she back to her days as a travel agent, recalling that since the breakup of the Soviet Union separate visas are necessary to travel to different regions of the country? She has some place in mind. But where? Does it even matter for me to try and make sense of time and place?

What I do know is that she is on the "border," the border between what is real and unreal, the border of the past and the present, the border of life and death.

Again she says, "How do we get out of here?"

"Where do you want to go?" I say.

"Do you have the vouchers, we need the vouchers," she repeats, becoming more agitated.

I look at her, see the anxiety in her face, and I experience her utter confusion. She clutches her walker and struggles to stand up. The word 'vouchers' is familiar from her days as a travel agent. At any moment her anxiety will turn to anger.

"If we're not in Russia, Mother, are we in Germany, are we waiting for a visa to America?" She stops for a moment with a look of recognition, as if she's thinking about what I just said.

I add, "Don't worry, I spoke to the lady and she said she would get the papers and then we can go."

A memory comes back to me.

I'm six or seven, living in the Föhrenwald Displaced Persons Camp in Germany, not far from Munich. It is 1950 and we've been in this camp for the last three years. I am sitting on a bench with my mother and father at the immigration office of a makeshift American governmental building, waiting to find out whether we have been granted a visa to emigrate to America. We enter a room where a man sits behind the desk looking at some documents. He's speaking to my parents. We leave the building. My father is solemn; my mother is distraught.

Is she waiting for the visa that she waited for back then, so many years ago, waiting for permission to leave Germany? Could that be why she is repeating, "How can we get out of here?" I've seen this look of anguish and anxiety on her face countless times, a frustration that led to desperation, then to hopelessness, as she waited. As we waited.

Her face has that same pained and worried look as she stands amidst the pictures on the walls, the old photos covering all surfaces that represent the remnants of her life, brought to her room hoping to ease the transition. Her anxiety becomes contagious and an old feeling of distress and guilt envelops me. As I was not protected from her pain in childhood, so it is today, as I stand here once again witnessing her distress in her room on the Alzheimer floor of the senior care center in Skokie, Illinois.

My mother, who rarely spoke of her parents or her sister when they were alive, is now wondering where her parents and sister are buried. Sarajane, the daughter of my best friends Annie and Warren, told me that on a recent visit my mother talked of Russia and of wanting to go home. She expressed her old lament, "I have no one." Sarajane tried to remind her:

"Babushka, there is Pips (my mother's pet name for me), remember Pips."

Sarajane is repeating the very words I would say to my mother as a child of nine or ten, when she would cry: "I have no one."

"But you have me, Mother."

Old, painful feelings, so many years later. I hear her words as I have heard them in the past… a plea to take away her unhappiness, a demand to stay near and never leave her, to do something about her pain, the pain of feeling she is an orphan, the pain of loss. And I also remember my anger at the demands on me and the guilt as I identified with her grief and sorrow. It was much later in life that I came to understand that no matter how hard I tried it was not in my power to make my mother happy. In the end she would always feel like an orphan, alone and abandoned.

My friend Susan keeps me company today while I visit with my mother. Susan and Annie are like sisters to me, the sisters I never had; we have known each other and each other's families since we were eighteen. Susan sits in her characteristic manner, concentrating and looking intently at my mother while biting the inside of her lip.

"Stop biting your lip, it's not good for you," I admonish, as I have done for all the many years we have known each other. Susan reflexively stops biting her lip.

"It's like we're waiting, waiting for Godot," she muses.

This sudden utterance is from the Susan I have always known, the one I took my first English Rhetoric courses with in college.

Samuel Beckett's play comes back to me in all its elusiveness and puzzlement, the endless waiting, the repetitive speech.

"When can we leave?"

"Is it time yet?"

"Go tell the lady."

My mother is Vladimir and Estragon, waiting in vain; the loss of the sense of time, the not knowing where she is or where she is going. The discomfort in her own skin as one moment she needs to sit up, the next to lie down, the dressing and undressing, putting on shoes, taking them off, scratching her head, her ear. Susan and I have also become Beckett's characters as we wait.

We watch her doze off. Her sleep is restless. Suddenly she opens her eyes and wakes to say: "Oh, you're still here."

We wait until it's time for lunch, and the three of us walk out the door and cross the hall to the dining room. On the way she stops the young, smiling dietitian coming towards us who greets her.

"Hello Sonja, how are you today?"

She replies, "How can we get out?"

The young women says, "Where do you want to go?"

My mother looks confused, has difficulty retrieving words, then finally says, "We have to leave."

Now, the dietician has also become a character in our drama and she looks bewildered.

I say, "She wants a visa to America." The young woman's smile freezes as if she has forgotten her lines.

" Have a nice day Sonja," she says, and she quickly walks away.

"What do we do now?," my mother asks.

"We have to wait until tomorrow," I reply.

"Why?" my mother asks.

"Because the woman says we can't go today. It is too late. Let's go eat."

Susan kisses my mother and fondly says, "Goodbye, Mamuchka, I'll come and see you soon."

My mother and I enter the dining room. There are no assigned seats for the residents, but my mother, who has persisted in demanding to be seated in the same place every meal, has managed to modify the policy. She takes her place in her familiar seat among the same five residents. Margaret, a German refugee from the war, is to her right. Despite her Alzheimer's we are able to converse, and she tells me that she was a baby nurse in Manhattan when she first came to America and later the administrative secretary to a college president. She wants to know what I do, and I tell her I'm a psychoanalyst. She smiles and says she is familiar with the profession.

The woman to my mother's left is pleasant-looking, well-groomed with beautiful thick silver hair. One of the aides on an earlier visit told me she had been a head librarian. I try to catch the title of the book she is holding in her hands but I cannot. She's always silent, does not speak to anyone and, as on my previous visits, she puts down her book only when the meal is served.

A third resident, Fela, speaks Polish. Fela is my given name and I think about how my name has undergone so many transformations and the accompanying confusion I felt, still feel, as my name changed upon leaving one country and entering another.

When my mother's food arrives, she doesn't want to eat. I try to coax her, but she shakes her head no and pleads with me.

"I can't…it's enough, I don't want. It's too much."

Slowly I seduce her into taking some bites. She mirrors me, offering me her food, wanting me to eat.

"Eat something," she insists.

At this moment the last thing I want is food. Nevertheless, in my attempt to get her to eat, I force myself to take a bite of what she gives me.

We are back in Beckett's play.

We sit at the table, passing the spoon back and forth, encouraging one another to eat.

A memory returns.

Reciting a Russian nursery rhyme, my mother feeds me. Her face is worried. She always thinks me a poor eater. I don't see it that way. I'm just particular about the food I eat. When I like something I eat well. I'm not interested in eating because I would rather play.

On impulse, I interrupt my attempts to feed her and ask: Do you remember the nursery rhyme that starts with, "*Ya tramvae yechali, sabaka, perayachali…*" (I'm riding on a trolley car and a dog crosses its tracks…)

My mother smiles and we take turns, each adding another phrase in Russian.

I was always puzzled hearing this nursery rhyme about a trolley car and the dog that suddenly runs into its path. What happened to the dog? Was it run over? But while this nursery rhyme always made me a bit uneasy, I enjoyed hearing my mother recite it in her beautiful, melodic voice.

I'm suddenly brought back to the present when I hear the voice of a Russian resident, loudly pleading, "*Mamushka, Papushka, sabri mye domoi.*" Momma, Papa, come take me home.

CHAPTER 2

Elizabeth's Story

It is early morning and I'm sitting at the desk of my country home in the Catskills, overlooking the Beaverkill River. I gaze at the tall hemlocks outside the window following the river below as it stretches downstream, and my eyes land on an angler standing in the stream. I watch him cast his line overhead, patiently waiting to see if his fly will seduce the elusive trout hidden among the rocks.

Reluctantly, I turn my attention back to the several large X-rays on the desk before me, showing the shadowy images of my father's chest cavity and ribs. They are the films of his original X-rays taken in Munich in the years 1949 and 1951. I scan them, trying to locate the scars left from tuberculous, but I cannot differentiate one mark on the film from another. My father, Rachmil Berenholc, was repeatedly denied a visa to emigrate to the US because of this supposed history of tuberculosis. The United States Government was not eager to give visas to war refugees hoping to enter.

Once again, I'm reminded of waiting at the immigration office in the Displaced Persons camp.

I am accompanying my parents to the immigration office. I am left sitting alone in a dimly lit hallway on a long wooden bench; my feet barely touch the floor. I swing my legs back and forth staring down at the floor or at the door behind which my parents are being interrogated about our visa application. I'm very impatient as I wait for the door to open and for them to reappear. Finally, they emerge with distressed faces. I jump up, my father takes my hand and once more we go home with nothing to show for the visit.

This scene will repeat itself many times over the six years we lived in displaced persons camps in Germany — going to the immigration office, waiting endlessly, being questioned by the authorities and once more denied entry to the United States.

In the aftermath of the war there were many American Jews trying to locate surviving relatives. David Kravitz, in Chicago, was one of these relatives searching for lost family members. His search resulted in finding my mother, his Russian cousin, in the Displaced Persons Camp near Munich, and he set the wheels in motion to bring us to America. In the winter of 1951, a radiologist at Billings Hospital in Hyde Park looked at my father's X-rays and determined that he no longer had tuberculosis. The Department of Immigration in Washington finally granted approval for our family to emigrate to the United States.

Among the papers we brought along from Germany I find this telegram:

BERENHOLC FOHRENWALD WOLFRASHAUSEN CALIFORNIA 21B US ZONE. INFORMED HEALTH SERVICE CABLING DISPLACED PERSONS COMMISSION RAHMIL APPEAL GRANTED CABLE COLLECT IF YOU NEED ANYTHING LOVE= KRAVITZ

Drawing a portrait of my father does not come easily; it feels much like trying to read the grainy X-rays of his lungs. He died in 1964, a week before the New Year, and my mother can no longer help me with his portrait. My father was a scarred man from childhood, beginning with the loss of both his parents in Poland when he was five years old. And while for me "Ray" evoked the sun's quiet, mysterious warmth, my father's Americanized name "Ray" could also be read as a representation of a life that began with an X mark in front of it. My father's silence about his life in Europe and his quiet reserve, which he maintained even with his closest friends and family, forced me to turn to documents carried across the ocean and stored in the drawers of a sideboard in my mother's home. But there is one other person who can help me fill in the history that my father could not speak of — his niece Elizabeth, our lively, loquacious family historian.

It is my mother Sonja's 87th birthday. My family and friends have gathered at the Lieberman Senior Center in Skokie, Illinois, to celebrate the occasion. In contrast to her strong presence before she entered the residence a year and half ago, her valiant struggle to cover up her worsening state of mind now appears very fragile. Ultimately, it became clear that her memory was seriously compromised. Her move from her home was long overdue but she stubbornly refused to use the help of a caretaker or to agree to move into an assisted residence. It took a fall, a hip replacement, and complications of surgery to make it necessary to transfer her to the Lieberman Senior Center.

The birthday celebration takes place in a spacious room with large windows that look out on snow-covered trees and rooftops—a Chicago winter. The room is comfortably furnished with a grand piano in one corner and seating areas where relatives and friends can visit with the residents. A large dining table covered with a white tablecloth sits near one of the windows. In the center of the table is a large birthday cake, ordered from a kosher bakery in accordance with the dietary rules of the residence. My mother, who now uses a wheelchair, is sitting at my side along with her caretaker Maria. She looks pleased to be surrounded by relatives and friends who have come to honor her birthday. My mother still recognizes me, but I see the quizzical look in her eyes as she stares intently at someone's face, trying to sort out the confusion in her mind. She is trying to recognize the people around the table who have come to celebrate her birthday, people she has known for the greater part of her life. The gathering includes my father's niece Elizabeth, the daughter of his older sister Sarah. There is also Elizabeth's daughter Francine and her husband Paul, my cousins Susan and Shar, the daughters of my father's younger sister Tema, and Shar's husband Rusty. David Kravitz's wife Bell is also here, as are my dear friends Annie and Susan whom I consider family. It is a noisy and boisterous group, catching up on each other's lives, exchanging news of growing children and grandchildren and discussing politics. Front and center sits Elizabeth in her role as comedian, telling her famous off-color jokes. She has a flawless ability to recall hundreds of jokes, stopping intermittently to grab someone's arm and laughingly say, in her Yiddish-Slavic accent with its rolling r's: *Can you believe it, it's so funny!*

I can't ever recall hearing a coherent story of my parents' past or for that matter of my own early life. I have never fully understood the sequence of events in the early period of the war that led my father and his family to leave their hometown in Poland and find themselves transported to Siberia. Nor do I know where and how my father and my mother met and married. Was I in truth born in Russia, as I was told many years after the fact? No official birth certificate exists, and my American naturalization papers state that I was born in Poland. Even before my mother's memory began its rapid decline, she was incapable of giving a coherent narrative of her life. I assume that the chaotic displacements during the war and the traumas she suffered in those years, including her separation from her own family, made recalling details difficult. My father rarely spoke about his past so he could not be relied upon as a source of information—although upon reflection, I'm not sure I ever tried to ask him. Recently in conversation with my cousin Susan, I asked if her mother had spoken of her past. Tema, my father's sister, would occasionally reminisce about her earlier life, but her daughter Susan was uncomfortable hearing it because she could not tolerate the pain her mother had endured. I wonder if the same were true of me in relation to my father. I sensed that his mysterious silence spoke loudly of his sufferings. Perhaps I could not bear to hear it, and I instinctively understood that asking him questions would open concealed wounds.

I'd intended for some time to learn more about my father's history. Preoccupied with my mother's fading memory and thoughts of losing her, I felt driven to learn more about my family, as if I needed to fill my mind with remembering as fast as she was forgetting. This gathering was just the opportunity that I'd been waiting for.

I look at my cousin Elizabeth at the head of the table, my oldest living relative who was present at my birth. I hope that she can provide me with the missing links that can answer some of my questions. Annie, who is sitting at her side and has her own deep appreciation and interest in family history, pulls out her iPhone, deftly taps the recording icon and begins to record Elizabeth's story.

With some excitement, I'm prepared to begin interviewing her. Words barely escape when I realize she is not listening to what I'm asking because she has her "own story" to tell. She announces that she wants to tell us how it happened that her name was changed five times. I'm surprised that this is her response to my desire to know the history of our family, and I wonder what this has to do with the questions I want to ask. It dawns on me that beginning her story with her different names is her way of creating an outline, of putting order to her uprooted, displaced, and traumatic early life. I'm reminded that I too have many name changes and do not own the name I was given at birth. As she speaks about her many names, I interrupt and point out a discrepancy between what she is telling me and what is written on one of the documents that I came across. She looks at me with a serious face and replies: *Everything is false. Well, I have five last names. Five last names. Do you see a story there?*

As I try to follow Elizabeth's disorganized telling of events, I'm once more aware of an old and familiar frustration, like the frustration with my mother when I tried to set down a coherent narrative of my family's whereabouts. But the difference here is that Elizabeth vividly remembers a great deal and she is a wonderful storyteller. Annie manages to record this attempt at an interview that is more like a free-for-all, with everyone interjecting comments and questions. My cousins Susan and Shar add bits of history relayed to them by their mother, Tema. The end result is a transcribed recording that reads like a rough road map, with many jogs and detours, a map that marks a journey where the travelers do not know why or where they are going or what they will find when they reach their destination. It is a journey that takes them through Poland, Russia, Czechoslovakia, Austria, and Germany and ends once they cross the Atlantic to America. Yet, despite the disordered and muddled telling of this tale, Elizabeth manages to give us a clearer sense of my father's early life and the experiences he endured as a child and a young man. As for knowing my father better, that still remains a question.

Elizabeth, now seventy-nine years old, begins her account with the family leaving the small village of Dlugosiodlo about seventy-five miles from Warsaw. I learned that in 1921, when my father was seven years old, the population of Dlugosiodlo consisted of 1,744 Poles and 801 Jews. The Jews lived in the center of the village near the marketplace and the Christians lived on the outskirts, adjacent to their fields. It was also a place that attracted vacationers because of the dense forests and pleasant climate. In the 1930s most of the Jews were merchants and peddlers in the surrounding villages. The village also had tailors, my father's trade, shoemakers, carpenters and blacksmiths who sold their products on market and fair days. There was a religious school and later a school built exclusively for girls.

As I imagine my father's village, I recall a popular Yiddish song called *Oyfn Pripetchek*, meaning on the shelf of a Russian cooking stove. The first stanza is about the love and joy of learning the alphabet. As a child I never tired of hearing this song with its hauntingly sweet melody and lyrics about a rabbi teaching young children the *Alef-Bet*, the Yiddish alphabet. I pictured a cozy room with a rabbi sitting on a chair, his young students sitting on the floor looking up at him as he told them a story. Maybe this song had a particular appeal because I grew up surrounded by wonderful storytellers, including my mother, who loved to read fairy tales and recite Russian poetry to me in her lyrical and dramatic voice. My mother's Russian education demanded that children memorize poetry, so she knew many poems from memory including her favorite poet Pushkin. As a young child I was not thrilled with Pushkin, but I have fond memories of sitting beside her as she recited some children's rhymes, often stopping and waiting for me to fill in the next word or phrase. One such nursery rhyme was called *Ryaba* the Hen. I still hear her voice, rhythmical and resonant as she begins her recitation.

Once upon a time there was an old man and an old woman, and they had a hen named Ryaba.

I would wait in anxious anticipation for her to come to the part where the hen laid not a plain egg but a golden one. I felt a great pleasure in hearing my mother read, in the same way that I enjoyed listening to the musical lyrics in *Oyfn Pripetchik*. Elizabeth, too, created an atmosphere of warmth and fun as the extended family gathered together listening to her, whether in the DP camps in Europe or later when we were in America. I look back fondly on the vacations spent together in rented houses or cottages on Lake Michigan or in Ontario, where Elizabeth settled with her first husband Sasha, also a young orphan and survivor of the war. We would sit up to all hours of the night listening to Elizabeth entertain us with her stories and jokes and I would experience the pleasure of family.

My father's extended family brought me a sense of comfort and security. Elizabeth's liveliness, humor, perseverance, and her sustained hopefulness served as an important model in the face of hardship, trauma, and loss. Her four children, six grandchildren and six great-grandchildren are a testament to the importance of family remaining deeply connected. It gives me pleasure to think of her children today sharing a cottage on a lake in Michigan, gathering together as we did those many summers ago.

So here we are once more all together, sitting around a table in the dining hall of the nursing home celebrating my mother's birthday.

My mother, still very slight and pretty, with flawless skin, her hair no longer bleached blond but now a lovely gray, her eyes still a beautiful green kaleidoscope of colors, gazes intently at Elizabeth and me. I can see she is trying to follow the conversation but she looks frail and confused, no longer her former emotional, determined, and opinionated self. I feel sad seeing her unable to express herself and add her stories, and yet there is something comforting and expectant as our faces turn to Elizabeth who, with her round, open face, blond hair, blue eyes, dressed in gay colors and customary gold jewelry, appears happy to begin her tale. We prepare to listen to her describe the events that led to her having five names.

Elizabeth's Story[1]

From Poland, where I was born, we went across the border because Poland was taken in 1939, half by the Germans, half by the Russians. Germans came into the town and it was September third. September first started the war. I was nine years old. And the planes were flying low. You could even touch them, they were so low. And they started to bomb, but it was a small town so they didn't really have to bomb. And the Germans walked in, a lot of them, and they knocked on every door and they said all the Jews should come out.

It was a small town so once a month we held like a flea market in the Rynak, a big, big market area. So they [referring to the Germans] got on the platform to make an announcement in this market. One German went around and was cutting the beards. And everybody was religious there - most of them were religious, with the beards, so he was cutting the beards. One side he left hanging and other side they cut completely.

My mother was holding me by the hand and I was like a towhead, completely blond with blue eyes. And my mother looked like a Polish woman, too. So the German —we tried to join the Jewish people and he told all the religious people to stand on their knees while they were cutting their beards halfway. And my mother wanted to join them so the German says, "You're not Jewish. Get away from here." So, my mother says, "Why are you doing this to the Jewish people? Why? He says, " We want to show in Berlin how those dirty Jews look like and we will show pictures in Berlin." And one was going around taking a movie.

And, in the meantime, my uncle was walking from schul. My father's youngest sister had four children and her husband was Aryeh Yosef. You wouldn't be familiar with it but Aryeh Yosef was a big deal in Poland. He was a very famous rabbi. And his son married my father's youngest sister and they had four children. And that's all he did is study; didn't do one day's work.

---

1   This is a transcription from the iPhone recording retaining the original syntax and grammar.

So, he was walking from schul with a prayer book and the tallit. You know, a tallit. And the German said, "Halt! Halt!" And he wouldn't and he shot him in the back. That's the first time I ever saw a dead body. That was right away, at the beginning of the war.

So, one German got up on the platform and he said like this: The Fuhrer does not like the Jews, they are worse than ants, they are worse than - they are worse than vermin. They are lousy. And if you want to stay, you can stay, but anybody can come and rob you and kill you and there won't be no punishment for that. That's it. So, the Russian border in Poland - the Russian-occupied - is still open. So go over there.

We packed up whatever we could, we dressed in layers, and we closed the door. There was no transportation. My grandmother, my father's mother, was the only one that owned a wagon and a horse because they had a store. Your father's parents, your grandparents (she turns to me), *weren't there anymore they died after the war* [World War I].

When I was in my teens, my mother told me that my father never got over being forced to leave his home in Poland to be shipped to a labor camp in Russia. When in 1946 a second amnesty was declared between Russia and Poland, my father insisted on returning to Poland. This was despite the difficulty of my mother being a Russian citizen. The mother of an eighteen-month-old, she did not want to leave but felt little choice. Parting from her parents, her country, and all that was familiar left her with that lifelong feeling of being an orphan, and the consequences of these losses reverberated throughout my own life.

Growing up, I was puzzled by my father's desire to return to Poland, especially since my mother often reminded me of Poland's history of anti-Semitism and complicity with the Germans. Even when we were well situated in the United States, I could sense that my father longed to be back in Europe and, unlike my mother, he never became fully comfortable or assimilated in the States. Listening to Elizabeth reminded me of the fact that as young boy he was orphaned at five, grew up without parents, and was forced to leave the only place he knew as home. How must it feel to close a door, leave everything behind, and not know whether you will ever see your home again? He left a significant part of himself in Poland, the part of him that felt real, where he belonged. Perhaps he was mourning this loss as I saw him moving so silently and mysteriously through his life.

As I write this, two memories come back. I'm seeing my father with his head bowed, slowly riding a bicycle, accompanied by his beloved dog Satan following slowly behind with his head also bowed. They are heading out of the DP Camp where the Great Dane, who has rarely left his side, will be permanently abandoned and turned over to a farmer. Satan is whimpering and I imagine tears in my father's eyes.

The second memory is at a train station in Germany. My father is saying goodbye to his closest friend, his cousin Lazer. We are about to board a train for Bremen where the ocean liner waits to bring us to America. My father is holding Lazer in a close embrace and crying as the train is about to pull out. I never saw my father cry, and I feel my own tears welling up as I write.

Elizabeth continues:

Tema and Ray and my mother and myself and my brother. I had a brother, Moishe. So we were starting to walk. My grandmother took a lot of her stuff, put it on the wagon. And she was very short; my grandfather was tall. And she loved jewelry so on every finger she had rings and she had a tiara covered up with gold chains. She was hiding it under the clothes. But while she was on the wagon this young German walked up to her and he says, Give me all your jewelry. And she says, Why are you doing this. What did we ever do to you? And my grandfather used to say, Ah, the First World War the Germans were much nicer than the Russians. Who wants to go to the Russian side? They are horrible over there.

So the young German says to my grandmother, "Give me all your jewelry and stuff." And she didn't want to give it to him so he took the bayonet and he hit her over the head. He killed her right away, and started taking the... Yes, right before my eyes. Yes, the uncle was shot in the back. Yeah, I went to the funeral. Yeah, right before my eyes. Yeah.

So my grandmother was killed right away. And her daughter was a young girl and she had four little children, little ones. Maybe the oldest was seven years old. So, you know, but they were religious people, they have a child every year. So they had four children.

And we started walking across to the Russians. We came to a town called Lonja. As soon as the Russians walked in they closed all private enterprises. You couldn't buy a piece of bagel, you couldn't buy a bread. The stores were closed. So now we are in Russian-occupied Poland. People started to get typhus. They couldn't wash their hands—there was no water.

So we were trying to trade something for bread. So my uncle, Moishe—you remember him—he went to trade a pair of pants for some bread and he thought a Russian soldier was watching him so we got scared. The middle of the night we ran away to Bialystok, because he was afraid to be arrested. Yes. So, we wound up in Bialystok. Moishe was married to my mother's sister the one who died as soon as we left and crossed the border to Lonja. Her name is Fegel, and Phyllis is named after her. She died of TB. She was forty years old.

Fela, Fegel, Felicia in Germany, Phyllis in America. As I hear the name of the dead aunt after whom I was named, I feel uneasy. I knew I was named after my father's sister Fela, but I knew little about her. Many in my family are blue eyed with blond or light brown hair, but I pictured her dark haired and ghostly, as if she were hovering above us. The discomfort at hearing her name must go back to my childhood, knowing I was named after someone who died young leaving four children, my cousins. My father and aunts never stopped mourning her death as a way to keep her close.

I suddenly become aware that Elizabeth is continuing with her story and I look up to see all the familiar faces from my past. I'm struck by the fact that we are all carriers of our shared fragmented histories and that my father and his sisters' fierce bond has been passed down to us, their children, who are now sitting around this table trying to piece it all together. Elizabeth's mention of the name Fegel also recalls her earlier remark: *Everything is false. Well, I have five last names. Five last names. Do you see a story there?* I do see a story there, and her words recall my own sense of uncertainty. I'm reminded of the day a year ago when I first moved my mother into the nursing home.

Going through her papers, I came upon a folder containing documents, fragile and yellowed with age, that my parents carried with them to America. Among these documents were papers signed by witnesses attesting to where my parents and I were born, where we were during the war, when they were married, a certificate from the Jewish organization ORT stating my father's occupation as an accomplished men's tailor, medical records, documents noting that my father was never arrested for criminal activity, visas to enter the United States from Germany, and vaccination certificates. It was in this pile that I also found the telegram from David Kravitz informing us that we had received clearance from the Immigration Department to enter the United States, as well as the 1958 naturalization certificates from the State of Illinois granting us United States citizenship. Once more I was reminded that I own no official birth certificate. Looking at these papers, I experienced a familiar feeling of searching for something. What was I searching for? I was aware of becoming impatient and not wanting to look too closely. I suspected that whatever information these documents held might pose more questions than answers, adding to my sense of confusion.

People meeting me for the first time sometimes inquire where I am from, and I find myself momentarily freezing. They ask because they hear a touch of Chicago accent. I hesitate for many reasons. First, I feel that any answer I give would be only partial, since I can't fully situate myself in any one place despite having lived in Chicago and New York for almost my entire life. I know that I'm not necessarily being asked where I was born, but that is the first thing that comes to my mind. My place of birth has been changed for the "official record," and so to say where I was born is to get caught in uncertainty, having been warned not to tell the truth about my place of birth. The question of where I am from conjures up another question: what country are you from? I don't have a name for such a country because I don't have a country where I can place myself. The answer that would feel most real is that I was born in the region of the banished people and this location happened to be called Russia, and I spent my early age from the age of three in a Displaced Persons Camp in Germany. However, since I don't think anyone would want to hear this after asking an innocent question like "Where are you from," I usually answer, "I'm from Chicago," which feels true enough.

I feel the same knee-jerk aversion when I hear my name—*Phyllis*—not because of anything inherent in the name, but because it does not feel like it belongs to me. I was born Fela Berenholc and, while I was uncomfortable being named after a dead aunt, it was my given name. In Germany, I was called Felicia, and arriving in New York it was changed to Phyllis Beren, depriving me of both my name and surname. I prefer all the many nicknames that my friends and family call me, Felichka or Fegela, Pips by my mother and Phyl or P by my close friends. I've always regretted not having taken back my original name. It is for this reason that I only fleetingly considered, then decided against, taking my husband's name, not wanting to add further confusion.

Looking at these old documents also brought me back to a time many years ago when I was twenty-five and first entered psychoanalysis. I told my analyst that I remembered little of my childhood before the age of eight, that my history was a jumble in my mind. I also hesitated telling him the actual place of my birth. When I was thirteen years old, my mother finally confided that I was born in Russia but warned me always to say Poland which was written on the naturalization papers. The revelation that I was born in Russia did not come as a surprise—my mother 's face never had a look of conviction when she told others where I was born. I sensed that I was not to probe more deeply, despite my own uneasy feeling. Children can both know and pretend not to know, taking their cues from the adults around them.

Incapable of offering a coherent history to my analyst, I decided to pursue more information and phoned my mother, determined to take careful notes this time. Pen in hand, I began by asking her about my birthplace. Why did we leave Russia for Poland? How did we wind up in two different Displaced

Persons Camps in Germany? Why did it take over six years before we could obtain visas to emigrate to America? Once again, she dutifully offered a history of our journey through different countries, cities, and towns. And as I listened to her and tried to jot down what she related, I sensed her bewilderment and confusion. When I looked down at my notes covering the entire page of my notebook, I saw before me an indecipherable script, words and sentences that began, trailed off, and included no punctuation marks.

I hear Elizabeth's voice and I shake myself out of my reverie.

So now we are in Bialystok—when we went to Bialystok my mother's, uncle—lived in Bialystok. So he took us in—my brother, myself and my mother. Bialystok was a very big town. Around the town were little summer homes. Poland had a lot of lakes and beautiful trees. It was beautiful there. So I used to run through a park to these summer homes and there was my mother's family, Ray and Tema, and Moishe's four kids—Leah, Shmilka, Manacham, and Aaron. The whole bunch was there. And then I was going to a Russian school already, in Russian- occupied Poland, and my brother, too. My brother was learning to become an electrician.

Her brother? I keep forgetting that Elizabeth had a brother and also a father. They were barely mentioned in the family. As I never questioned where the truth lay about where I was born, I never asked about her father. It was particularly noteworthy because I only knew Moshe to be Elizabeth's uncle and then stepfather after he married Sarah. Elizabeth always referred to him as her uncle, *Feter* Moishe. Here too, despite it being explained many times, I was left confused about out how he could be both her uncle and her father

So what happened… every day after school I used to run through the park to visit my relatives. I used to go visit them and they would sit there in the cabins, they had a good time. It was hard to buy bread, it was hard to buy anything. So they were trading, they were playing the black market—whatever.

One day I go there and the whole place is a ghost town. It was locked up with nails. There was nobody there. So I'm running back and I come to where my mother lived and I said, "Mama, Mama, your brother is gone, your sister is gone. There was nobody there." So she says, "What do you mean?" and she says, "Nobody is there. It's closed." So my mother started screaming, "What happened? Who took them?"

An hour later a Polish boy came on a bicycle and Moishe gave him five zlotys, which means like five dollars, and he brought us a note. And the note said like this, "In the middle of the night the Russians came and they took us away. And we are in such-and-such station. And come to some cattle trains, like where they're taking cattle. And we're all on that train. So tear up your passports"—we already had Russian passports—"tear up your passports and come where we are. Whatever will happen to us will happen to you. Come on the train. Leave that place." So what happened was we tore up the passports and we went to the train. My mother's father's uncle with who we were staying decided to go back to their homes in German occupied Poland. Where they were now they couldn't get bread, they couldn't get water. Typhus started to go around. So they said, "What are we doing here? The German-occupied Poland, we have beautiful homes there. Why don't we go back to our houses?"

Susan, you are asking if they knew. They didn't know what was happening. I am sure some of them read Mein Kampf and everything but they—I don't know what was wrong with those Polish Jews. They said, "Let's sign up and go back to the house." But the border was closed already. So all those people that signed up to go back to Poland, the Russian government pronounced them as enemies of the Communist regime. And we were taken as political prisoners. We were taken all over Siberia—some went to Siberia, some went to Arkhangelsk Oblast. Yes, Phyllis you are right, The Russians didn't mean to but they saved our life.

So while we were at the train in the cattle cars, my mother overhears them talking and they say like this: single people, they're going to send to different camps; married people to different camps. So my mother didn't want to be separated from her brother and her sister, so she took on her maiden name—the name of Berenholc. So we became Berenholc. So at home I was Michler, my father's name, and getting on the cattle trains, I was Berenholc. So I have already two last names.

Our trip took two months, by the time we got there. Fegela, (Elizabeth turns to me), *you want to know about my brother. My brother was on the train, and then he says to my mother, "I'm learning to become an electrician. What's the rush? When you get settled down I will come to you." And he jumped off the train. And my mother was holding him. It didn't help. The train was already moving. He jumped off the train; we never saw him again.* (Annie, recording what she just heard, asks, "What year was this?"). *In '41 I think the Germans killed him, as soon as they attacked Russia.*

The song *Oyfn Pripetchik* again enters my mind. Elizabeth's story is no longer just an attempt to make coherence out of a disjointed history, nor is there comfort or amusement in the telling. Her matter of fact, unemotional tone belies darker feelings. The feeling of comfort I first experienced at being gathered together has dissipated and the song, unlike the first stanza that conveyed the joy of learning, carries in the fourth stanza a disturbing, sinister message. *When, children, you will grow older/You will understand/How many tears lie in these letters/And how much crying.* One view of the song suggests that the lyrics hint at the traditional Yiddish saying—*The history of the Jews is written in tears.* I now feel this in Elizabeth's recounting of what happened to her brother. Her face shows little emotion, her tone is more subdued, and her eyes have a faraway look, as if she is once more living the scene of her brother disappearing in front of her eyes.

An eerie silence falls over the room. We are all feeling the horror of her brother jumping off the train, his mother trying to hold him as his body slips away from her, never to be seen again.

Anyway, so we went and the place where they took us was called Archangelska Oblast which is close to Finland and we could hear the Finland war. When Finland had the war with Russia, we heard the artillery and the shooting and everything. So it wasn't quite Siberia but it was way up there and it was as cold as Siberia. It was seventy below zero, sixty-five below zero. And in the winter the snow was so high. And if I went to school there, I had to go on cross-country skis, in the winter. We were all the way up north by the Northern Sea. Did you see Dr. Zhivago? When she goes through the blizzard? That's how it looked. Oh yes, (turning to my cousin Susan who asks about clothing), *they gave us clothing. They gave us sheepskin coats and sheepskin boots. And most of the people went to chop the trees. The trees were so huge, the trees. They were cutting lumber. And they were using a saw, two people, but it wasn't an electric saw. No such a thing. Axes and saws.*

I hear in Elizabeth's voice and see from her face that she is far removed; back in the vast, deep, hidden forests of Russia, seeing it all over again, the final destination, the cattle cars disgorging their unknowing travelers. Images of her life there rapidly tumble out as she describes this faraway, cold, inhospitable, snow-filled landscape.

"We call this Siberia," Stefan Waydenfeld writes, "perhaps strictly speaking this is not quite true, but in a way it is. Siberia is not just a term out of a geography book applied to northern Asia, it also means a place of internal exile. Here we are still in Europe, not in geographical Siberia, but it is certainly a place of exile, it is the political Siberia." (*The Ice Road*, p.101)

The idea of thinking about Siberia as not just a geographical place but a place of internal exile spoke loudly to my confusion about the place of my family's deportation. I would add to the idea of *'internal exile,'* also the idea of *'eternal exile.'* It also explains my intense obsession with scrutinizing the various maps of Eastern Europe, trying to locate the spots on the map where their journey began and ended. The task was futile and impossible. Looking at the maps I would see the borders moved and the names of towns changed, reflecting ever new occupiers. My mother would often refer to where I was born as "not exactly Siberia."

And they only had five grades over there. So I went to school and the rest of them went to chop wood. My mother rode a horse. The horse was pulling the logs. Tema worked in the bakery and she used to bring a little bit of flour so we had a soup. They had one restaurant over there that served to the ones that produced the most amount of lumber. It was called stakhanovites; you wouldn't know what that is. Stakhanovites means they produced more than their quota. Means surplus. So they got an extra piece of bread and the borscht that they served was cabbage soup and everybody got a wooden spoon and everybody ate from one bowl. So it was - we were hungry there a lot. In the summer we survived a little better because the summer was just daytime, no nights. Three months. And there were a lot of raspberries growing and strawberries, and blueberries. You could sit at the raspberry bush for three, four hours and not pick everything on the bush. It was—and my mother used to make—what do you call it?—raspberry syrup and jam and stuff like that.

And they had the bread—they used to cut the bread. We lived in log cabins. We had such big ovens and there was a platform and I used to sleep on the platform from the oven in the back. That was my room. Tema and my mother slept in one bed and Ray slept in the other bed. In the middle was a table and it was wooden floors. You had to take off your shoes and they washed the floors, with a special knife they cleaned the floor—the wooden floors. It was all wood over there. And the ovens were so big, like you—you could cook—you could shove in the whole cow, it was so big, the oven. And I remember she made sliced potatoes and on the door from the oven, she made like cottage fries that you eat here. But it wasn't with oil or butter, just dry. It was delicious. And my mother used to go out in the summer and look for all kinds of weeds, like herbs or something, to add to the bread. And as soon as she baked it, we ate it up. Because we were always hungry. The only fish they brought in there was white fish from the Northern Sea and it looked as big as a whale and they were cut into pieces, but they had to soak them maybe for five, six days to get the salt out of it. It was so salty. And then they prepared it. You ask if we ate animals. In the woods were bears. Mostly bears. White bears and brown bears used to look in the window. We didn't eat bear. Once a brown bear killed a person there.

So Annie, you are impatient to know if this is the same place as where Phyllis was born. Oh, no, no. I am coming to that place. I'm coming. This is in 1939, we stayed there until 1942.

Listening to Elizabeth's description of the place my father rarely mentioned, I'm being given a lens to view this geographic wilderness. I can finally see the bleak accommodations that were my father's home for nearly four years after leaving Poland. I glance at Bell Kravitz, eighty-eight years old, her silver-gray hair perfectly arranged, still wearing her signature high heels, and I see that she is looking mildly uncomfortable. Born and raised in a small American Midwestern town, she drove over today in her 1960's baby-blue convertible Cadillac, a gift from her deceased husband. I wonder what she makes of this storyteller and of the relatives her husband located in the DP camp and brought to the New World. What do any of us make of this? The endless hunger produced by the starvation diet, the bitter cold, and the forced labor. Yet, despite it all, I hear immense courage in Elizabeth's vibrant voice, and I see resilience in her lively blue eyes and face as she evokes the images of the sensual pleasures—the crusty bread, the delicious potatoes, the berries, and her mother's jam. I'm in awe of her abundant capacity to experience happiness in the face of such enormous deprivation.

My parents also had a great deal of courage and resilience. It was only in passing that they spoke of the time in Russia, so I was unaware of the brutal picture that Elizabeth had now drawn. Not having been told where in fact I was born, yet suspecting it was Russia, I drew a romanticized picture of my birthplace from the stories I heard. In my mind's eye, I saw a storybook village of small, neat houses surrounded by green fields. Our family proudly owned a goat named Tzig Tzig and much was made of this beautiful white goat with a bell around her neck, contentedly chewing grass and offering up my drinking milk. My Aunt Tema loved recounting stories about how smart the goat was, and how she came running when her name was called. I imagined the village with one road leading to a large town where my parents walked to work, my father sewing uniforms for Russian soldiers, my mother teaching at a school and my aunts staying home to take care of me. Perhaps this picturesque scene was further stimulated by my mother's stories about her childhood growing up in Russia, images that would capture my imagination; a cat curled up on a large stove in her home similar to the one Elizabeth described. My mother would tell me with pride about the skis her father made by hand, with which she travelled to school over the deep snowy-wooded terrain of the Russian landscape. Like Elizabeth, my mother's eyes would light up with pleasure as she spoke of the delicious blackberries and the *yablaka* or apples that she could pick off the trees and bushes in the yard.

The impression I received about my father's family home before they were forced to leave Poland came from Elizabeth and from my mother when I asked about the family name of Berenholc. That home was surrounded by lakes and forests. The family name might have its origin from my great-grandfather who was said to have been an overseer of the woods (*holtz*) on a Polish estate. Growing up, I heard that the family had some means, that my grandfather owned his own wooded land and sold lumber. There were seven siblings—four brothers and three sisters. The oldest brother lived in Warsaw with his wife and five children—all of them killed during the war. Another brother died young in an accident, another followed his communist girlfriend to America and died when he was thirty-nine. Fella, the eldest sister, died shortly after the family had to leave their home in Poland, leaving her four children behind. A few of the siblings continued living in their large home after their parents died within a year of each other. When my father was five years old, his mother died giving birth to Aunt Tema. Not long after, my father was apprenticed as a tailor. Elizabeth's mother, Sara, rented out the main room, the size of a ballroom, to a dance teacher for his lessons. Elizabeth was an excellent dancer and loved to dance.

When I began high school my parents bought their first home in Chicago. I remember feeling surprised and curious as my father quietly went about planting flowers in the boxes on the veranda, tomatoes and vegetables in sunny spots in the backyard. I had no idea that gardening was of interest to him, until I remembered that stepping into Tema's living room in Chicago was like finding yourself in a light-filled greenhouse.

I realize now that forests played an omnipresent role in our family. The woods surrounding their homes in Poland and Russia offered many pleasures—picking berries, apples, foraging for mushrooms, picnicking and swimming with friends in the nearby lakes and rivers. The forests were places of forced labor and unbearable cold, but also a potential space where they could flee and hide to save their lives. And as I discovered most recently, they played a major role in how my parents met. But that comes later in the story.

I'm looking around the room of the senior residence, the winter sun filtering a warm glow through the large windows, the table now covered with the remains of uneaten fruit and the last of my mother's birthday cake. My mother, dressed this morning by Maria in an attractive sweater with her famous long nails manicured and polished as always, sits beside me. I'm amazed at her green eyes, her beautiful unlined skin. My cousin Shar frequently joked that she wanted to know the moisturizer my mother used to make her skin so flawless. Her face at this moment is turned to Elizabeth, intently looking at her, straining to listen. From time to time she reaches for my arm, turns to me and asks, *What is she saying?* How do I explain? I tell her she is talking about the time they all lived together in Russia and she nods. The answer seems to satisfy her, but I see in her expressionless face that she can't understand or follow what is being said, because otherwise I would hear her fervently adding commentary in her once forceful voice. Little of her voice is now left.

But what of my father, which is where the idea began of asking Elizabeth for an oral history of their life? I see him as a silent figure, like his shadowy X-ray, standing in the background. Is he less present because I lost him when I was twenty—forty-five years ago? Or is it also a function of my mother's personality which was always in the foreground? Are some of my memories too painful to keep in mind? I am certain that the feelings I have for him run very deep.

I recall his lively, brilliant blue eyes and his open smile, inviting and warm. Although short and thin, he appeared substantial. Early photos showed him to be exceptionally handsome. As he aged, I saw a resemblance to Humphrey Bogart. Maybe it was because he wore a trench coat similar to by Bogart in *Casablanca*, one of my favorite films.

What I mostly associate with my father is his devotion to his craft as a custom tailor. I remember watching him create custom-made suits in the store he owned in the Chicago suburbs. He made beautifully tailored clothes for my mother and for me, some are still tucked away in my closet. On our walks along Michigan Avenue with its exclusive department stores, he would pause to examine the newest fashions on display, then take a small notebook from his pocket and quickly sketch the outline of a suit or dress that my mother pointed to.

I remember him at other times as I gazed at our two reflections in a full-length mirror, myself erect, him kneeling deep in concentration, a tape measure in hand. I can still feel his hands on my body taking precise measurements of my waist and hips, then turning the tape vertically to measure the length of the imagined skirt, the tape stopping slightly below the knee. I can still hear him admonishing me to stand straight and be still. It felt like an eternity, this measuring business. But choosing the fabric for the skirt always gave me great pleasure. From shelves holding fabrics, he would take bolts of woolens in different colors and patterns; plaids, herringbone, tweeds, and solids, then spread them out on a worktable for us to look at and choose. My love of fabrics of unusual and unexpected textures must have come from him.

I was transfixed watching him draw a pattern on paper and then on muslin to create a silhouette of the garment. When he made a suit jacket, he would baste the pieces of muslin together for a first fitting to make sure the measurements were correct. Once satisfied that the muslin fit, he readied himself to cut the fine fabric with his large shears, and when that was done to sew the pieces together. During the second fitting, he was prepared with chalk in hand and straight pins between his lips to make the adjustments needed for the garment to fit just right. The suit jacket would remain on the manikin for a last try-on. When he worked he always wore a tie with his shirtsleeves rolled up. His cigarette hanging from his lips, sometimes in an ebony and silver holder, he bent over the sewing machine or work table where he was cutting or basting, his fingers deeply engaged, not noticing the ashes falling on the cloth that was to become a jacket, pants or skirt. Quickly and deftly he brushed the ash off the garment, putting the cigarette in a nearby ashtray and continue his labor.

His thimble seemed like a permanent part of his finger, his large clothes brush always close by to brush and remove any suspicion of lint. The fabrics he chose were always the finest English woolens or imported silks. My mother used to quote him as saying, "We are not rich enough to afford poor clothing." When I felt the urge to have a new a skirt or dress I would plead and cajole, making a nuisance of myself until he finally acquiesced. I always felt it to be a loving gesture on his part because I knew how busy he was filling orders for customers. He was creative and perfectionistic in his ability to personalize the garment to fit the body. When he finished a garment, he would take visible pride if "it fit like a glove," and he was known to tear an entire jacket apart if he saw it did not fit well, no matter how much time he had already spent on it.

Another memory that is dear to me: I was in high school and my father agreed to make a Halloween costume, a flapper dress of a light blue shiny material. He first made a simple shift and then cut out what seemed to me a multitude of three-inch bands of the same fabric, and attached these horizontally one under the other over the length of the dress. Using pinking shears, he cut strips to hang vertically from each horizontal band. I remember that as my body moved in the dress, I had the feeling of being surrounded by rippling waves.

I recall his curiosity about a new product on the market called Velcro. He had just finished a pleated skirt for me, but instead of the customary zipper he had substituted Velcro. I remember admiring how ingenious that was, how he was not afraid to experiment with something new. His talents were admired in the family, among friends and by his customers. His craft was the one area of his life that he could depend on to give him a sense of confidence and continuity.

All these memories of my father flashed through my mind in a moment and were suddenly interrupted by Elizabeth's description of life before my parents met. I turn to her as she continues with her story:

Then there was a General Sikorski who was a general in the Polish army in exile. He lived in England. And he made a pact with Stalin to let the Polish citizens go, to let them out of Siberia. "They are not enemies and they are not criminals." So finally, they let us out from there. We thought we will never leave that place.

Susan, you are asking why we were sent there in the first place? We were sent to Siberia as political prisoners, against the Communist regime. Because in Russia-occupied-Poland some of Jews signed up to go back to Germany. To their homes in German-occupied-Poland. We didn't sign up to go back but most of the people did over there, but they sent us there too. We [the family] had torn up our Russian passports so they thought we were traitors. Traitors against the Russian government. Traitors, because some wanted to go back to German- occupied Poland.

Anyway, so what happened was they [the Russians] *let us out and most of the refugees from Poland, they went to Asia - Tashkent, Georgia, West Pakistan. And I said I'm not going there; let's go where Lenin was born and the River Volga.*

Elizabeth is now very animated as she describes how she chose the town of Ulyanovsk, Lenin's birthplace, as the place where the family should go. My cousin Susan interrupts to ask how old she was and when Elizabeth replies that she was twelve years old, Susan looks incredulous and asks, "Why would they listen to a twelve-year-old?"

As this exchange takes place, I wonder how she has retained this particular memory of her role as the one responsible for such an important decision. Has this memory been reworked over time, reflecting Elizabeth's determination not to be defeated by adversity but to keep her gaze towards the future and survival? Does the memory serve as an example of a young girl forced to grow up prematurely, compelled to take on enormous responsibility in the face of the powerless adults she sees around her? The memory is also a window into her remarkable character, her innate liveliness and her exuberance. She wants to go to the birth town of the famous revolutionary Lenin, the man she learned about in school, the man she admired.

Stefan Waydenfeld, in the *The Ice Road*, relates how the Poles were granted amnesty and told to fill out forms stating where they wanted to go when they left the labor camps. His family sat around looking at the forms and had no idea where they should go. They had been cut off from all news about the war and what was occurring outside the labor camp. Stephan suggests that the family leave for either Astrakhan or Tashkent; Astrakhan because he remembers the delicacy of the caviar he ate in Poland before the war, and Tashkent because he is reading a novel, *Tashkent, the City of Bread* by Tolstoy. The adults are pressured to make an important decision based on little or no information and are paralyzed. But adolescents can still dream and imagine. They dream of caviar, bread, and revolutionaries; the adults knowing no better can only shrug and go along.

And so, based upon awakened feelings for her revolutionary idol Lenin, Elizabeth suggests that the family leave the labor camp for Lenin's birthplace. Youthful enthusiasm has always been part of her character yet, sadly, after the loss of her beloved husband Sasha to cancer when she was in her early forties, her optimism was shaken and I have noticed a paralysis grip her whenever she has to make any decision. Of all the losses she had to bear, his loss was one too many.

Elizabeth does not answer Susan's question, "Why would they listen to a twelve-year-old?" She continues: *Anyway so, and every time the Russians said to me, "Why don't you become a pioneer"? No, Phyllis, your mother's different—she was in the junior party of the Communist organization.*

Elizabeth's allusion to the difference between my mother's and her relationship to the Communist Party reminds me that almost all young children in Russia joined the Young Pioneers, which began as a scout organization introducing the values and goals of the Soviet Union, offering educational and recreational opportunities and indoctrinating children into communist ideology. My mother was originally a Young Pioneer and would have officially become a member of the junior party of the Communist Party because her father was a card-carrying member of the Party.

We weren't allowed to settle. The Russians said we weren't allowed to settle in Moscow, Leningrad - well, Stalingrad was destroyed completely. In the big cities, we weren't allowed to go. So where we could go? So where did we go? To a town called Vishkima Rianaski Oblisk, near Ulyanovsk, and the county was Kuybyshev. You heard of Kuybyshev? It's called now Novosibirsk. It just used to be Kuybyshev. And the River Volga. Okay? And we settled down.

We lived in one house, maybe 500 square feet, it was one room and two beds with a table in the middle. Your father, Phyllis, right away got a job. Got a job sewing for Russian soldiers or something. My mother got a job. And Moishe lived in a different house with the four kids. And my mother and Tema and Ray lived in one house.

Then I went to school—the Russian school—and all of a sudden one day the Russians came and they took everybody and they put them in jail. Why? They wanted to force us to take Russian passports and the family said, "No, they will never let us go to Poland again." And they want to go back to Poland. So two hundred were put in jail- and imagine, I was the only Jewish girl in the Russian school and they used to look at me like crazy. Everybody was in jail, I was with the dog at home, and I used to go to jail and say, "Mama, you need to take the passport. Take already that trashy passport; you'll have to take it anyway."

When Elizabeth mentions jail I hear a buzz around the table and see everyone looking at one another, bewildered and asking questions about what happened. Why was she not put in jail? Elizabeth explains she was too young to be put in jail because she was only twelve or thirteen. Once more she explains that the Russian authorities wanted the Poles to take Russian passports, but the Poles refused because they feared not being allowed to return to Poland.

I see that it is impossible to gain a linear narrative or coherent picture. The changing political landscape of the moment dictated the policies and laws that affected millions of dislocated people, no different from our world today. And we around the table are also reacting to the uncertainty and confusion stirred by Elizabeth's story, trying to make sense of it, yet aware that it makes no sense. Still, these stories remain our most valuable history, despite the futility of ever really knowing the whole story, whether it be the story of my family or the countless others who were affected by the war and the many who lost their lives.

The buzz continues and the questions keep coming.

So everybody was in jail for two weeks. Was I alone? How did I buy food? Did I have money? What kind of money? My mother prepared enough food. We had a goat—we had a goat there. And we ate—and listen, that goat gave milk. Sonja used to pump her own breasts to leave for Phyllis's milk. And I got up one morning, I was rushing to school, there was a glass of milk and I drank it. So I drank her breast milk. Ah, it was so sweet.

Annie asks, "How did Phyllis's parents meet?" Elizabeth looks surprised by the question and a bit distracted by the interruption in her narrative.

I think in Ulyanovsk. I don't know why he went there. Somehow Sonja came from Gomel and she met Ray and he told us that he met a very beautiful girl. And then all of a sudden, they got married. That was it.

My friend Susan says, "That's it?" And laughs. "That's it? That's what we have been waiting for?" I'm also wondering why Elizabeth does not say or know more about how my parents met. Was it that as a young girl she was not that interested in how they met? Perhaps everyone in my father's family was also in the dark about how they met and married. My parents never told me the story of their meeting or of their marriage. Of all the many photos I have there are none of their wedding. There is obviously more to the story.

My cousin Susan asks Elizabeth if she knew my mother's parents.

I knew Sonja's parents. Of course, I knew them. And I knew her sister Riva too. Sonja was teaching. She....I think she had a few years of college. She was a teacher. So I know that she was teaching in Russia, she was teaching literature in Ulyanovsk. And so Ray met her and he brought her home. And that was that. And then you were born.

At last, I ask Elizabeth when I was born. I turn to look at my mother who either does not hear the question or is lost in her own mind. I sense that what she mostly wants is to be safely by my side, celebrating her birthday with me alone. It must be tremendously confusing to see familiar faces engaged with one another while she herself is uncertain about who everyone is.

"When was I born?" I ask again.

About nine months later. And they finally got out of jail because they had to take the passports anyway. They became Russian citizens. And then in 1946...

It's clear that Elizabeth wants to change the subject. I always suspected my parents got married because my mother became pregnant. Recently, I discovered an official document from Germany stating that my parents were married in 1948, which would mean that my mother gave birth to me when she was twenty-two. That is, of course, if her age on the official documents is correct.

So Phyllis, Elizabeth continues, *you were born a Russian citizen.* Susan's face shows doubt and questions my being born in Russia. Elizabeth's adds, *I know that it does not say that on her passport.*

Annie relates how when we were in college during the Cold War, I told her and Susan I was born in Russia, but that they were not to tell anyone. She was surprised that it was a secret. To this day I feel uncomfortable about all the fabrication. Yet it feels good to have a witness to where in fact I was born.

No, Phyllis was not born in the Russian-occupied Poland. She was born in Russia, whatever her mother wrote down is false. They changed it. Yes Phyllis, you were born June 13, 1944, 1 think in our town outside of Ulyanovsk. I think in a hospital, there was a hospital there. As a matter of fact, I know there was a hospital because my best girlfriend was Lublila was a midwife.

We left Russia in 1946 after the war was over. We were on trucks and they were going back to Poland. You ask if we knew what was going on. We came to Poland and we found out about the concentration camps. We came to a town called Klotzko, which was a border with Czechoslovakia. And we moved in—Yes, Sonya came. And Phyllis was there and my mother. And Moishe and his kids were somewhere else, in a different place. But we were all together. Ray and Sonya and Phyllis and my mother and Tema. We were all together. So we moved into a house that was so beautiful, in Poland. And they had-they must have been collectors of stamps- because there must have been about three albums. If I would only take those albums of stamps I wouldn't have to worry. They were beautiful. But then we found out about the concentration camp—we didn't know in Russia. We didn't know what happened to the Jews. I found out my brother was shot. I found this out in Germany. I didn't know before that.

So, what happened was we paid—we joined a Jewish organization in the town we were in Klotzko, near Czechoslovakia somewhere. We didn't move to Israel but we joined an Israeli organization—a real religious one—because they came from Israel to sign up people—young people—to go to Israel. They were trying to promote everybody to go to Israel. My mother says, "You are not going to Israel because you are going to go to the Israeli army and I lost one son already. No, no Israel."

When we were in Poland we found out that a lot of people lost their life even after the war. So we signed up to be smuggled through the Russian border into Czechoslovakia. The Russians took Czechoslovakia. I came to Bratislav and I stayed there three months, until Sonya, Ray and Phyllis joined us. We didn't want to leave without them. It was Czechoslovakia, occupied by the Russians. So I helped my mother and I helped when a lot of Israelis came to churches to buy off and get back some Jewish children that were left behind and the parents never came back. So they took transports of kids and they brought them through Czechoslovakia. And I remember my mother and I helped to feed them. We worked in a restaurant, like volunteers. So I met one little girl, she was wearing a big cross; she was raised in a Catholic church. And she had a mark where she was shot. Her name was Ursula. And I said to her, "Aren't you happy? You are going to join your family in America? And you are going to go back to being a Jew." She said, *"Get away from me, you dirty Jew."* Like that, just like that.

We stayed there for three months, until Sonya and Ray joined us, and Tema. We waited until we had the whole family together. We got on the train and we went to Prague. And from Prague we went into Germany. We were smuggled across the borders in the middle of the night. Phyllis spoke Russian and her mother tells the story that she stuffed a handkerchief in her mouth that night so she wouldn't speak out and they would not hear Russian. Right, so that the Soviets wouldn't shoot. That was going from Poland into Czechoslovakia. But while we were in Czechoslovakia already we went to Prague, and from Prague we went to U. S. zoned Germany. Susan, you ask where did they take us? To Ulm Un Danau. Ulm, near Stuttgart, Germany. And we stayed in Ulm.

So what did they do? They took two streets - the DP camps. They took two streets and they emptied it out of the Germans who slept there. They were the barracks of the Germans. And we occupied their homes. Sonya and Ray lived downstairs, we lived upstairs. Fela and Aaron - Aaron brought over Fela from Poland. They just got married. And I think Rebecca was born there. And she was already - she was already about three years old, I think. Rebecca was Moishe's granddaughter. She's the one that has that lingerie store in the Village that was on the program Sex in the City.

Elizabeth turns to me and says:

Phyllis you were maybe two years old or almost three. I have pictures of you. You were so beautiful. Oh, my God. I was as a practical nurse in the camps. I finished school in Germany.

Reminded by Elizabeth that she was a practical nurse I interrupt her: "I have this memory that you took me along to the clinic because you had to work. While you were sterilizing needles, I was playing with them. I don't know if you remember this, but I was having fun playing with the needles and then of course I wanted to use one to give you an injection. I gave you a shot, and you yelled at me. You came running after me but didn't catch up until I had arrived home. My mother always said I was a very fast runner. I think I was three."

Elizabeth continued:

Oh, you were—wait. I finished nursing school—I finished nursing in '48. You were about four years old. Yes. And I worked in the other camp. Where we lived was called Bleidorn-Kaserne and where I worked was Boelke-Kaserne. And there was another DP camp called Donaubastion-Kaserne, and Sedan-Kaserne. And we lived in number 777 Kaserne in Germany.

We came from Ulm in 1949 to America. My mother married Moshe in '48. 1 said to my mother, "My father is still alive in Cuba." My father was in Cuba through all this. So my mother says, "I lost my son and it is his fault." Moshe was married to the older sister Fela who had died and was left with four children. He wanted to marry Tema, but his children were almost the same age as Tema. Anyway, 1948 came and my uncle wants to marry one of the sisters. If not the younger one, the older one. He doesn't care. He is not going to take a strange woman.

Moishe's sister lives in America. He writes her a letter and he tells her to get somebody to go to Cuba to find my father, he should sign the divorce. And that's what happened. Someone went to Cuba, found my father and had him sign the divorce. By the way, my father and Moishe were first cousins. My father went to Cuba when I was six months old. He didn't want to go to the Polish army and his mother sold everything and she sent him to Cuba. And people didn't make a living in Poland at that time. It was very hard, before the war. And she never saw him again, 1930 he left. So what happened was that friends of ours, from our hometown now living in New York went to Cuba and found him. And he signed the divorce and then the divorce came right away. They got married in 1948 and in 1949 we got the papers for America. It was a problem because Moshe had four kids and my mother had one child. So because she married him he would have to do adoption papers, which would take us another three years in Germany. So he said instead of having four kids, he had five kids. So I became Greenspan. Number three.

Elizabeth looks subdued as she is speaking about her father, at the point in her story where she has yet another name change, "number three." I feel the pain of her father's loss, a pain she has carried all her life despite never having known him. I again am struck by the anguish of the family situation; her paternal grandmother did not want to lose a son in the Polish army and so she sends him away, with the result that my aunt loses her husband and her children are left fatherless. More recently, Elizabeth told me that after a time in America she wanted to go to Cuba and visit her father. My father discouraged her because he was angry at this man who had left behind his family, had in essence abandoned them. The theme of loss is so omnipresent that I find it quite unbearable to contemplate. I begin to understand why it took me so many years to want to know more about my father.

Then I came to America, I got married. It was Dell, the fourth name. Then my husband died. I re-remarried, there was Silver—fifth name. Five last names. Over there they didn't change the names officially, they just acknowledged it. Or change a number, erase a number and—I was always afraid that the Americans would find out that I came under a pretended name. My mother's name was Berenholc. My mother's parents had property, they were cutting down lumber and sending it to America. The grandfather had money and one of the uncles was very wealthy in Warsaw. Five kids he had. The Germans killed them— my mother went specially—she paid a guide to go from the Russian-occupied Poland to Warsaw to try and get him out. And he wouldn't go; somebody was sick. They were killed. They were so handsome, my mother's brothers. I can't tell you. Like Ray, he was gorgeous. I have a picture of a brother from California that died—that came before the war here. Thirty-seven, he was when he died.

Elizabeth has a dreamy look in her eyes as she speaks of my father and her handsome uncles. But then she looks fatigued and stops speaking.

After a short silence, my cousin Susan relates a story about her mother, Tema. "My mother tells the story, when they were getting ready to leave Poland when Germany invaded Poland, the Germans came into this small town that—my mother had a little ice cream/candy store. There was a Jewish holiday that was going on so people from out of the area were in the town at the time, because they were getting ready to go to this Jewish holiday. When Germany came in with the soldiers, and they gathered everybody in the town's one meeting place, in the center of the town. They said they wanted everybody there. And they said, 'If you are a Jew and you're not from this town, you've got to leave right now.' In other words, get yourself out of here. 'If you are a Jew and you live in this town, you've got twenty-four hours to pack your things and get out.' So, my mother, at the time, who looked very Polish, was very confused. She didn't understand what that meant, because this was the start of the war, when they were invading Poland. And she goes up to one of the Germans and she says to him, 'What are you talking about? What do you mean we have to leave?' And the guy says to her, 'Just Jews.' She says, 'Well, I'm a Jew.' And he slapped her. He slapped her so hard she fell to the ground because he didn't believe she was a Jew and she was claiming she was. So I remember my mother telling me this story. Then she said one of the uncles—one of her—no, maybe it was a family member, but it wasn't her uncle—was starting to run and they told this old guy—'Stop!' The guy was deaf. He didn't hear; they shot him."

Elizabeth's voice:

It was my uncle. My father's sister's husband. They shot him in the back. He was walking from the synagogue. Someone said, 'Why did you shoot him? He couldn't hear.' And they said, 'He's better off.' And they just killed him on the spot.

Susan is struggling not to react and proceeds with her story.

"So my mother tells the story of how they had to go back and decide what to take, because now they have to gather things. My mother said they left a pot of soup on the stove in the kitchen. And my mother and Leah—Moishe's oldest daughter, only a few year's difference in age—takes this wringer of the washing machine and my mother asks, 'What are you going to do with the wringer?' And she says, 'Well, you never know. It may be worth some money. You know, we could buy...' Now, the good news was that my mother and Leah didn't look Jewish. They were very blond and very Polish-looking and they spoke some German and they spoke fluent Polish, so they got away with it. Well, the German soldier thought that they were confiscating some weapon, because he never had seen a wringer thing. And they detained them for hours while they explained that this was just a wringer. Such strange stories."

We have all fallen silent, deep in our own thoughts. An unfamiliar, Slavic-looking woman approaches our party pushing a resident in a wheelchair. The woman greets my cousin Fran, whom she recognizes from their volunteer work as docents at the Holocaust Museum in Skokie and introduces the older woman as her mother. We all stir, disoriented, as if we have awakened from an unsettling dream and look at the strangers in our midst. My mother, startled and becoming agitated, points to the newcomers; "Who are they?" While practically silent throughout Elizabeth's narrative, she is now alert. Perhaps she felt some comfort that we had all joined her in the past, where she now resides. With the intrusion of these strangers she announces, "Let's go, Phyllis." My mother's birthday celebration has come to an end with the countless "strange stories" of an unimaginable era.

Elizabeth, Ulm DP Camp

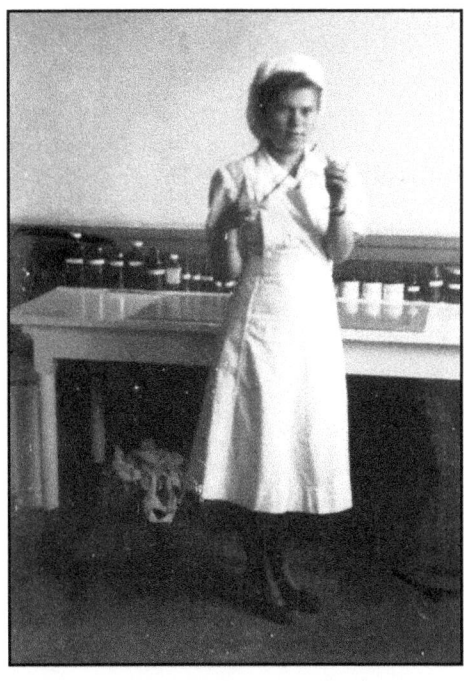

Elizabeth as Nurse, Ulm DP Camp

Elizabeth on bicycle, Ulm DP Camp

Father's family with Sarah & Elizabeth on the right,
Tema on the left. Mother directly behind Father; I'm in his lap

CHAPTER 3

My Mother's Story

Two years later I woke up very early one morning and remembered it was Mother's Day, I made a mental note to call my mother later at the Senior Residence. Earlier that week I'd decided not to send her a card as I had done all the previous years, knowing that this year she would not be able to read it or even comprehend that it was Mother's Day. Instead of the card, I would send a bouquet of flowers, hoping their colorful blooms would bring her a fleeting moment of pleasure. While she still recognized my voice on the phone, it was only a matter of time before this too would fade away like her memory. Maria, her caregiver, had taken to answering the phone, placing the receiver next to her ear and in a cheery voice would say, *Sonja, it's your daughter Phyllis, here Mama.*

When was it that my mother decided to write about her life? It must have been at least five years before she broke her hip and entered the senior residence. From time to time, she mentioned she was writing a story. When I asked what she was writing, she would only say, *what I went through*. At the time I did not take her intention seriously; she frequently had ideas about what she would like to do in the future. I encouraged her in her plans, but she would just as quickly find some reason why she could not do it. Nevertheless, when it came to her writing, I continued to urge her and ask to see what she had written. She would put me off with, *I'm not finished*. As I look back, I wonder if I should have pressed her harder. Perhaps, I restrained myself because of my own ambivalence about wanting and not wanting to know.

It was after she had been in the residence for over a year and it became clear that she would not be going home that the time came for clearing out her house and putting it up for sale. In a drawer of a bureau filled with a jumble of objects and an assortment of papers, I spotted her unmistakable handwriting on a few worn sheets of paper. I was once more struck by her elaborate old-world handwriting, with its letters precisely slanted to the right. How different it looked from my own unschooled script. Among the sheets was one typewritten page on the back of a fax she had received in 2002 that looked like a copy of one of the handwritten pages. Could it be a clue to the date she'd begun writing this piece? In typical fashion she had recycled old sheets of paper.

I picture her sitting on the wobbly black swivel chair in her makeshift office, the chair like her slanted script tilted to one side. For many years I recall being astounded by her obliviousness to the chair's precarious condition, that she could easily slip off the seat and land on the floor. But my fears never materialized because once seated she always righted herself. Her reading glasses rest unsteadily on her nose. She holds a pen in hand and her head is bowed over the many papers that clutter the round, dark brown veneer table. I see her shuffling through the pages of what she has written, checking and rechecking them as I have seen her do with her bank statements.

Adjacent to the kitchen is a small, cramped room that serves both as her office and eating area. Sitting down for a meal with my mother, I would first have to struggle to move the heavy swivel chair on its chrome base across the deep piled Moroccan carpet, a hand-me-down from me to her. The carpet was really meant for a study or bedroom, but she insisted it belonged in this room where it awkwardly lay. The walls bear the busy orange and mustard-flowered wallpaper of forty years ago, its pattern broken only by a display of my stepfather's paintings and drawings. Nothing in their home has been changed since he died more than twenty-five years ago. An imposing blond wooden breakfront, separated from its rightful place in the formal dining room, takes up one side of the room. The surface of the breakfront is covered with a crystal set of matching glassware brought over from Germany sixty years earlier; a wine decanter with six glasses rest on a cake plate, a fruit bowl and nut basket complete the ensemble. The bureau is home to stacks of papers pertaining to her work as a travel agent, bills, occasional cards, and junk mail. Several drawers hold personal and financial documents, cancelled checks, photos, letters and cards from family and friends. The remaining drawers are filled with table linens, including several brought from Germany. A record console of blond wood from the fifties sits against the other wall, and on it rests a manual Cyrillic typewriter that my mother uses for correspondence with the Soviet Union Inter-Tourist Travel Agency. A window in the room looks out on a large tree, its branches touch the window pane, and from time to time she allows herself to be distracted by the visits of the songbirds to the neighbor's bird feeder. Her beloved companion Verushka, a Russian Blue cat, is often curled up on the chair next to her.

On Mother's Day of 2011, I bring myself to read what she had written. The process of reading my mother's story is no easy task. I'm overcome by a familiar frustration as I try to decipher her dizzying handwriting. I examine the numerous drafts like a detective. At first glance, they all look similar, as if she simply copied what she wrote on a number of different pieces of paper, then typed a final draft. However, on closer inspection, I see sentences scratched out and rewritten, and I struggle to untangle these changes. The source of my annoyance is not only the mechanics of making sense of her writing; it is the frustration I've felt my entire life in not having a coherent picture, call it a map, of my origins, of the place where I was born. This frustration frequently shows itself in impatience, a character trait of mine that I don't particularly admire, an impatience that comes over me when I feel confused or thwarted. It was only later in life that I understood there was good cause for this intolerance. Only when I reached adolescence was I told the true place of my birth, but the circumstances that led to the deception remain a mystery. To this day, as I look over my parent's early documents and research the war years and our immigration to America, new discoveries unfold. But my questions only increase.

Finally, I reached the conclusion that my mother was indeed attempting to write a story that was meant for others to read. It seemed a fitting gift to celebrate her on Mother's Day—to transcribe the story that she put to paper, and to honor her wish to write *what I went through*.

Gathering up the separate sheets before me, I will now attempt to assemble the pieces of my history, this time with help from mother's story.

The story takes place in 1945–46 and is an account of the time they spent in Poland after leaving Russia. I have kept her sentence structure and spelling as written. To my knowledge she never studied any formal English grammar, beyond a few classes in conversational English that she attended with my cousin Elizabeth taught by a British woman in the DP camp in Ulm. Many of her words are spelled phonetically. For example, she writes the word occupation as 'accupation.' At times her spelling reflects some German influence, when she writes "inwited," instead of invited. Yet, when she arrived in America she was fairly fluent in spoken English. She also spoke Polish and German and was pleased to tell me that she studied some French in Russia along with German. She only began to speak some Yiddish after I was born, while living with my father's family. She had a distinct Russian accent when she spoke English.

Belonging Nowhere: by Sonja Kaplan Berenholc

It all began with the end of the war.

We belonged nowhere, nobody wanted us. We were given repatriation papers, sent to a small town in lower Silesia, Glatz, close to the Chech border.

The apartment we received was in a very nice section of town, was accupied predominantly with German and Polish people, in fact we were the only jewish family there.

Glatz, as it is known now as Clatcko, because of the Polish accupation in accordance with the Yalta Conference, was at the time a very nice, clean town, somehow hilly, full of green, with nice houses, and people going around free.

Most of the jewish people were resettled in the lower part of the town, street named Nizka.

There were very few German people left in town, it was rewarding to see them wearing yellow armbands, rewarding in a way, that made them stand out and being looked upon as outcasts the way they did to us. It did good for our ego.

The apartment building we occupied, belonged to a German artist, who broke a leg and could not leave town. They had an apartment on the upper floor, actually the attic, as the rest of the building was accupied with Polish tenants. Downstairs was a German bakery, now run by Polish people. The bakery was full of fresh bread, rolls, pastries, which was quite inconceivable to us, when for such a long time we only dreamed about it. Although the food was rationed, one always found a way to obtain something extra.

The apartment we lived in, once belonged to a German doctor, once huge, was divided into two apartments, joined by a corridor. The front part was occupied by a young polish woman, who was a little hard of hearing, the result of brutal bitting (beating) in the concentration camp. We became very friendly. She was a very beautiful and intelligent woman, a bit mysterious, often visited by high ranking polish officers. She lived alone, her fiancé fled Poland after the war avoiding the Russians and resided in England and was in the Polish provisional government in exile. He was an officer in the Polish Army, belonged to an aristocratic family, and so was the neighbor whose name I cannot recall. Her dream was to get away from Poland, away from the Russian accupation. She actually could have gone, but I do believe she was working for the Polish underground army, as she always had visitors coming to her apartment at odd hours.

Once, quite late in the evening we heard somebody knocking at her door for some time. When I went out to see who it was, I encountered an older, very distingwished gentlemen, who introduced himself as the Father of the lady's finace. We inwited Him to our apartment where He stayed overnight and we did not close our eyes all night watching him. We noticed that He put a gun under his pillow. It was a very stupid thing to do, to invite a stranger in. Nobody was safe in this unsettled time. Early in the morning when we heard our neighbor in the hall, we told her about the visitor, who was indeed her future Father in Law, we found out about her deafness. From then on we became very friendly with one another and she told us about her tortured times in the camp.

The summer of 1946 was in a way a peaceful summer. We learned how to relax and started to enjoy life a little bit more. The biggest attraction at that time was to go to the market, where you could get and sell anything you wanted.

One day I went to the market with my little daughter. She was a very active child and as children do wanted toys which we could not afford. In the market she spotted a woman selling a doll and of course she did not want to go away. My sister- in- law was watching her but somehow my sister in law turned her head and my little girl disappeared. The first reaction was to go in the direction where the doll was. But she was not there. The terrible panic, how do you find a little girl in such a dense crowd. Suddenly a friend of my husband's came up to us and said that two women grabbed my girl. We started running in the direction where he saw them, and to our horror we spotted two women, one of them carrying Phyllis and trying to board the bus. I spotted a policeman, thank God he was jewish. As they were about to board a bus the policeman stopped them. The crowd gathered around us, and the Lady holding Phyllis insisted she was hers. We had a very hard time getting my baby back. You must understand that after the war there were hardly any babies and one was always in fear that somebody can steal your baby. I made sure after that incident never to let my baby out of my sight. As a reward we bought her the doll.

Life was peaceful for awhile, it was actually as something unbelievable, to be so good. Well, it did not last and then it started all over again. One morning our relatives came running to us, telling us that a pogrom is in process. The Polish underground army and the bands of polish patriots who revolted against the Russian occupation, started to prosecute the jewish populations. They stopped trains, took off the jewish travelers, some of them they killed, some were badly beaten up. In Keltc, they entered an apartment of a high ranking jewish officer, who fought in the war in the Polish Army against the Germans, and killed him in the presence of his wife and children. Panic broke out, among the jewish populations, as they started to cross the border to Czechoslovakia.

We did nothing and did not know exactly what to do. To establish ourselves in Poland, start all over again or to move on. One felt uncomfortable.

One morning the bell rang in our apartment. When I opened the door a Polish officer questioned if jews resided here. I was so terrified that I slamed the door. I did not know at that time that my husband was expecting him and that made a deal with him.

That same night a bunch of drunken Polish people broke in to the apartment of the German architect who lived on the 3rd floor and brought out the whole family outside not letting them even put on shoes. We gave them the keys from the laundry, where they spent the night. Shortly they immigrated to Germany.

A week later a pogrom almost broke out. Most of the Jews who returned from Russia after the war lived on the other side of the town. The streets there were very narrow, the houses belonged before to the lower class Germans. My husbands relatives lived in that part of town. With the concentration of so many jews in there it became a Getho in some way. Among them lived a Polish woman, who besides speaking a perfect German, spoke a fluenty Yidish, telling everybody that her husband was jewish and perished in concentration camp. Her name was Wanda, and she was accepted in every Jewish family in the little Getho.

Passover was approaching. Everybody was getting ready to celebrate the holiday. Early in the morning she came out in the street shouting that the Jews killed a polish boy, for blood was needed for the Passover matsos. Luckily somebody alerted the police and luckily that particular group of policemen consisted of Jewish boys. The pogrom was avoided.

The Brecha [an underground Jewish organization] bought off the Polish guards on the border. We all assembled in a house close to the border waiting for trucks to pick us up. We had nothing with us, no food for my baby. Somehow my husband did not get on the truck, being a gentleman when it was announced women with children to go first. But some men did not obey the Polish police and threatened not to move. We came to the border, and the guards that were supposed to let us go by but they wanted more money, we thought the Israeli police already paid them already. Finally were allowed to cross border. We started to walk, Phyllis in my hands fell asleep. The road was very narrow in between on both sides rivers. It was very dark. In front of us was a man. I held on to the back of his jacket with one hand and carried my baby with the other. We walked about 1 mile until we saw the same truck already there. We crossed to the Chez side. They picked us up and we came to a camp.

Reading my mother's account is terrifying and yet, strangely, I feel little emotion. Is it because I grew up with these stories and thus they feel like the familiar scary parts of the fairy tales that my mother read to me? Or is it that I have read so many other stories about others who survived the war, and this one becomes one more story to add to the multitude of stories told and memories recalled? But I know better. My feelings of detachment signify the lasting effects of this early history, the need to distance myself from feelings of fear, pain and loss—the elements of trauma. In the place of strong emotions, I'm flooded with questions. Why, late in life, did my mother choose to write about this particular period of time when she left Russia for Poland? Why not write about the events that occurred prior to her departure from her homeland, such as her childhood growing up in the Soviet Union? Or why not write about her family leaving her hometown of Gomel before the Germans invaded the city? What was it like for her to give up her university studies and to move with her family to Ulyanovsk? How did the family live in Ulyanovsk and what did they do while they were there? Will I ever know the real story of how she met my father? Why did we live with my father's family and not with hers? Her story contains no clue to her mysterious marriage to my father, their relationship, her pregnancy, my birth, let alone her childhood, the war or her departure from Russia. Instead, my mother chooses to describe the town of Glatz, Poland, close to the Czechoslovakian border where we lived for nine months.

In the chaos and confusion of war, people are swept away by events over which they have no control. Has she repressed or sought to deny everything that went before? Perhaps those years settled like a fog on my mother's mind, the traumas she suffered becoming repressed memories, something like my detached feelings in reading her story.

In 1945 my mother left her parents behind in Russia. Until 1964 when she *found them,* she did not, in her words, *know whether they were dead or alive.* Leaving her parents behind in Russia was summarized by: *I'm an orphan.* I heard the lament *I'm an orphan* throughout my life as a narrative of her sense of aloneness, of her difference from my father and his family and even at times from me.

Throughout my childhood, I would also frequently hear these words: *I lost them, I can't find them,* and one day in the year 1964, *I found them.* What did my young mind make of such statements? How can one lose a mother and a father? They did not die, so how could they get lost? I recall having a sense that my mother left them behind in some faraway place. And maybe I was judging her for having done so, since I could never imagine leaving her and my father. I also recall thinking the opposite, how could her parents let her leave? It was all a mystery to me. Perhaps that is why I loved fairy tales and especially Grimm's tales of wicked people who kidnapped children, of children separated from their parents or of parents who died. These stories terrified me, yet I felt compelled to hear them read or told over and over again, like I wanted to hear the tale of my abduction in the market. Like the happy endings in fairy tales, my story held the reward of the return to my parents and the desired doll, but I also longed to find my grandparents, to see my unhappy mother and her parents finally reunited.

In her narrative, my young mother strikes me as intelligent, possessing an inquisitive mind. She is a keen observer of her surroundings, her description of her diverse group of neighbors comes to life on the page. She possesses an adventurous spirit and a capacity for pleasure. One instance of this is captured in her description of becoming friends with this *interesting Polish woman.*

In her story, my cousin Elizabeth noted that when they were in Russia they had little knowledge of what was happening in Poland or of the atrocities that the Germans were inflicting on Jews. But once in Glatz, my mother seems well aware of what occurred and continued to occur. She writes about anti-Semitism, pogroms, and the camps. Her story highlights for me the contradictions in her strong and determined character. My mother loved to argue politics and had a lifelong interest in current affairs, an interest that is seen in her story. She was clearly aware of the continued persecution of the Jews after the war ended. She often remarked that the Poles were as anti-Semitic as the Germans, but she also acknowledged that there were Poles who were resistance fighters, like her neighbor, who spent time in a prison camp. She writes about the Germans forced to wear armbands like they had forced the Jews to wear during the war. *There were very few German people left in town, it was rewarding to see them wearing yellow armbands, rewarding in a way, that made them stand out and being looked upon as outcasts the way they did to us. It did good for our ego.* However, when she speaks of a neighborhood being a "little ghetto," it sounds like a foreign experience to her. While she is well aware of ghettos, her writing once more indicates how deeply she is a product of the Soviet Union, where religious practice was prohibited and identification as a Jew was discouraged. I often hear her repeated refrain: *I did not know I was Jewish until the war broke out and made a Jew of me.*

It is also interesting that the Poles, Germans, and Jews in 1946 are living together in the same building, yet the persecution of the Jews is still rampant. She is sympathetic towards German neighbors when their apartment is broken into and they are forced out into the street without shoes by some drunken Polish people, and she writes of how they helped the family that night. She vividly conveys the mood of post-war Europe—everyone in terrible straits gripped by fear and uncertainty. And she identifies with her German architect neighbor and his family who are also displaced. *We belonged nowhere, nobody wanted us.*

I try to picture myself in her place at her age, separated from family and the mother of a two year old. Her adolescence and young adulthood were shaped by the war, and her life as a young university student was derailed by the war, forcing her to grow up before her time. It is curious how little my father is represented in the story. He seems for the most part absent. I have no sense of their relationship. Her narrative supports what I always suspected; were it not for my birth, she would have remained in Russia and most likely not have gone with my father to Poland. I recall asking her: *Why did you have a baby during the war?* And her reply: *You were an accident.* I believe that the guilt and heavy burden I have felt throughout my life in my relationship towards her began with my birth and was transmitted and reinforced in me by her sense of guilt about leaving her parents behind. I became responsible for separating her from her family and her country and felt it was my responsibility to make up for her losses, to remain by her side. This feeling of responsibility was reinforced by her often repeated words: *You are all I have.*

My mother was open about the fact that she was not prepared for motherhood as her pregnancy came as a surprise. She knew little about taking care of a baby. I'm fairly certain she took pleasure in me, but I imagine she must have been relieved to have my father's family providing the care. Perhaps this also has something to do with why she was living with my father's family and not her own.

At the start of her story I don't picture her as having a child. She sounds more like a young woman trying to regain the life she left behind, such as finding a friend in the Polish woman with whom she could feel comfortable.

Could the kidnapping episode have been a turning point for her—a dramatic awakening that she was no longer an unattached young woman but a mother with a child living in a dangerous world? Here again she vividly portrays the scene of panic, with everyone running in all directions trying to find me. She refers to me by my Americanized name, *Phyllis,* in the voice of the observer distancing herself emotionally from the experience. Once I'm found she uses the more personal voice and calls me *my baby.* I can feel her terror. She refers to me as her *little daughter* and describes aspects of my personality: *She was a very active child and as children do wanted toys which we could not afford.* She is not critical, but rather sees me like other children, wanting things. And I can hear her plaintive voice explaining to someone she imagines is accusing her of neglect, *You must understand the time. After the war there were hardly any babies left and one was always in fear that somebody can steal your baby and the women insisted that the baby is theirs. I made sure after that incident never to let my baby out of my sight.*

Was it after the kidnapping that my mother became more aware of loving me and decided never to let me out of her sight? Was it after this event that she become overly protective, unusually anxious, and worried about my safety? She dealt with her anxieties by becoming possessive of me. She was reluctant to let me go on sleepovers at friends' homes. I had to plead to go away to college and not to remain at home attending a local school. When I managed to convince my parents and left for college, only then did she show pleasure in my growing independence. Was I living the young student life that had been interrupted for her?

After the Keltc incident it became clearer that my family had to leave. *We did nothing and did not know exactly what to do. To establish ourselves in Poland, start all over again or to move on.* She was not aware that my father had already made the decision to leave, had actually paid someone to help the entire family cross the border into Czechoslovakia. Knowing what a difficult decision this must have been for my father given his strong desire to return to Poland, it saddens me to think about their relationship and my mother's inability to be more appreciative of the role he played in her life. But here again, perhaps it would have meant being able to face and acknowledge her traumatic past.

She ends her narrative in June of 1946, when the family crosses the border into Czechoslovakia by way of Austria to Kasel, Germany. In September we arrive at the DP Camp of Ulm in Donau, Germany. Many harrowing details about the midnight escape from Poland are left out. While she writes about my father being a "gentleman," and letting the women and children go on the first truck, what she does not write about are the subsequent events that I heard her retell as I was growing up, one more scary fairy tale.

I picture my mother carrying a heavy young child with blue eyes the color of her father's, wearing a fur coat with a matching hat. Her arms feel heavy with the weight of the child as she leaves Russia, dutifully following her husband back to Poland. Her young face has a pained and frightened look as she steps over an unseen line that is the Russian border and leaves her parents, her sister, and her friends behind.

I was only eighteen months old; it is not so much a memory but an image that has stayed in my mind, one that is a composite of my mother's stories filtered through her feelings and the photos I've looked at all my life. In one of those photos, taken when I was older, I am wearing a fur coat and matching hat. Perhaps this photo is what stimulated the image. Perhaps crossing the border from Russia to Poland has become conflated with the time when we crossed Poland into Czechoslovakia. I was two-and-a-half at that time. It is conceivable that I have a trace memory of this event. In my imagination, I picture her carrying me across many different borders.

It was a dark, rainy, and stormy night. She was separated from my father and was left carrying a very heavy child in her arms. She became quite hysterical when she learned that my father was not on the next truck. She tried to go back, but was urged on by the others and not allowed to return. As she carried me on a narrow path along a river, I suddenly yelled out in Russian that I had lost my shoe, forcing someone to stick a sock in my mouth. This is the story I heard recounted by Elizabeth. They feared the Polish guards who were paid off to let us pass would hear Russian spoken and shoot at us. We spent the night in some makeshift tent, with my mother crying until the next morning, when were picked up by another truck that would take us into Germany. My father finally met up with us a day or two later, but those two days were unbearable for my mother.

As a young adult I came to understand that the events of that night in 1946, crossing the border into Czechoslovakia, represented one of my earliest traumas. My mother's panic and my own fear at seeing her inconsolable would be replayed at other times of change, separation and dislocation in my life.

In the bureau where I found her story, I also discovered a box that contained another page with my mother's handwriting, another story she had begun to write that I had read before. Its words still sear my memory.

My mother wrote:

The story I am remembering started before the war was over. My mother after many years found her brother in Brestlitovsk, which at that time belonged to Lithivenia, then to Poland and finally the Russians took over. She went to see him. And when she came back, she arranged for me to meet my mother's brother, his wife and 5 cousins. I arrived there and I remember that my uncle told me: "Thanks to Russians they liberated me from my business, house and money." Naturally I could not understand this as I never spoke Jewish. So he explained it in a broken German, which I learned in school.

The Germans arrived there, they conquered Poland and put us all in the camp—actually a cinagog (synagogue).

We had Jewish police and one day they approached me and asked if I would go out (outside the town) *with one man and try to get some food as we were starving.*

Two days later we came back. The cinagog—camp was burned down together with the people. My uncle, aunt and 5 cousins perished.

We ran away to the woods. One priest made us false papers. But it became <u>*very dangerous.*</u> *We were told to go to the Germans for verification. We ran away to the woods. Met some partisans.*

Being alone, I married the man Ray Berenholc.

This page of my mother's writing sheds light on something I once heard that puzzled me. My parents were having an argument and my father, in an uncharacteristically angry tone, alluded to having rescued her, as if reminding her of some history between them. Despite my trying at a later time to question them about this, neither one seemed to want to talk about it. Could this have been how they met? In the woods when my mother was on the run? Was my father a partisan? From what she recounts, she clearly needed rescuing. Sadly, it also suggests that, at least on my mother's part, theirs may have been a marriage of convenience, as were so many marriages during the war. But I also can imagine that my father was truly captivated by this beautiful, educated young Soviet woman who needed his protection. And this is what I know about how my mother and father met.

On Mother's Day I'm thinking of my mother with her vanishing memory, her increasing dementia and her inability to recognize familiar faces. The person she most frequently invokes in reverent tones is my father. He is still there for her. She is waiting for her final rescue.

That night I dream that I'm on a trip to a foreign country that seems slightly familiar, Eastern Europe today. The buildings look old and ponderous. I am going back there with my mother and father. I leave a hotel with a strange name that I can't pronounce, a street name that I can't remember—some Slavic sounding name, not Russian. I leave the hotel room alone to go off exploring. I want to get back but can't find a taxi. I want to use my cell phone to call my parents, but I realize I left it behind. I see my mother's worried face. They have cell phones but I don't remember the numbers, I can't remember the name of the hotel and I don't speak the language. I stop at another hotel, ask the concierge for help and try to explain that it is an old hotel starting with an E. He gives me three numbers written vertically on a piece of paper, like Chinese characters on a page, 1,2,3. It seems strange. I try the numbers and I get a busy signal. I tell him it can't be and he gives me three other numbers. I get through but the person on the other end of the line can't understand me.

The scene changes. I'm on some tour with my friends, Annie and Warren and other people. While looking into stores, I'm separated from them. I see a narrow staircase down to a lower level where people in chairs are waiting for a lecture. I decide this is not interesting and try to climb back up the narrow staircase and find it very difficult. I continue up to the top and finally get out. I still can't find my friends. Against a wall, I see my green bag and on top are two old sweaters that I have discarded. I think to myself no one has taken them but I decide to leave them; perhaps someone will want them. I pick up the bag that contains some rumpled workout clothes. I remember that I had left my other bag, phone, and jacket on the floor. I find them and am surprised that no one has stolen them. I try to use my phone to call my friends but I can't get the phone to work. Again, I'm trying to get back and can't find a taxi. Two women come over to me and tell me that they will take me where I need to go. It's a car that becomes a van. One of the women gets in front and the driver seems to be someone she is intimate with. Two other men get in the car. I don't know them. I try to make room and then we are off.

    I wake up and don't want to think about this dream. I lose things and then I find them again. I'm being kidnapped once again. I still can't reach my parents or my friends. It all seems to be too much. I wonder if I really want to continue writing this memoir?

CHAPTER 4

Behind the Iron Curtain

It is a late summer afternoon in 1962. I'm sitting in our living room in Chicago, the door to the balcony open, hoping for a cooling breeze. I'm looking over the packet of information for the fall semester of my freshman year of college, and I am startled to hear the sound of the doorbell. Opening the door, I see my mother, returned from work earlier than expected. She is standing rigidly, her feet fixed at the threshold, an eerie smile on her face and a faraway look in her eyes. She stands there staring at me. In that stare I recognize a look of disbelief and I hear my own disembodied voice: "You found your parents!" She nods and as if she has seen a ghost, slowly moves into the living room, heads toward the couch, collapses on the seat and breaks into sobs.

How have I intuited this remarkable event? And what am I to make of this news? Stunned, my head spinning, I feel the rush of intense emotions, disbelief and wonder. Unbalanced, I sit down next to her.

My mother was nineteen years old in 1941 when the Germans advanced into Russia and took over Gomel, Belarus, the town where she was born. Just before the Germans gave orders to round up and shoot the Jews, she and her parents and sister fled east and relocated in the town of Uylanovsk on the Volga River. In the ensuing eighteen years after leaving Russia in 1946, she lost all contact with her family despite repeated searches through Jewish organizations and the Red Cross. My mother frequently expressed her profound sadness and loneliness in what became a mantra of my childhood, *I don't have a family, I have no one, I'm an orphan.*

I fervently watched the TV show, "This is Your Life," a reality documentary that played in the nineteen-fifties. Ralph Edwards, the creator and host of the show, surprises guests in the audience by taking them through a retrospective of their lives. I imagined myself such a chosen guest, invited to sit on the couch of the set. I sit in anxious expectation as Ralph Edwards holding a 'red book' in his hands proceeds to read my biography. In a voice filled with excitement and dramatic fanfare he announces and calls out one person at a time—friends, acquaintances, relatives—and at last my missing grandparents appear from behind the stage to greet me. They stand hesitantly while I try to recognize their faces. And as in *The Winter's Tale,* when Leontes gazes upon Hermione and she suddenly springs to life, my grandparents and I come towards each other in a united embrace.

My Uncle Lebel repeatedly told a story about me as a child of four in the Ulm DP camp in Germany that was meant to demonstrate what a clever child I was.

My father's oldest sister, Fela, who was Moishe's wife, passed away just when the family was forced to leave Poland for a Russian labor camp. Afterwards, Moishe wanted to marry Tema, Fela's youngest sister, but my father was opposed to the marriage because Moishe was considerably older and already had four children. So instead he married Fela's middle sister Sarah, but when Tema later married Lebel a fierce rivalry developed between the men.

I adored both of my uncles. One day in tears I came running to Lebel and pleaded with him in Russian:

Uncle Moishe told me that if I continue to love you, he will no longer love me, so promise me that even if I can't love you, you must love me still. Harosho, harosho? (Do you agree?).

Having been tutored by my mother from a young age on the subject of loss, the story suggests that in order not to lose the people I love I need to be very clever and persuasive to make sure I lose no one.

Now, sitting with my mother after her startling announcement, a rush of thoughts come swirling into my mind. I raise my head to look at her and wonder what to make of this news that she has found her parents. She is no longer an orphan and I, who grew up without grandparents, discover that my long-lost grandparents have reappeared. *This is my life.*

My mother worked at an agency that had one of the few contracts with the Russian government allowing travel between the United States and Russia and for material goods to be sent to relatives. As an assistant manager, she translated documents from Russian to English and English to Russian and spoke a number of Slavic languages. She was also the agency's merchandise buyer, recommending goods for clients to send to relatives for their own use or to be sold on the black market. This was the era of the Cold War; dealings between the two countries were highly restricted. In later years the agency came to specialize in Eastern European travel, and my mother's voice could be heard on Chicago's local Russian radio station advertising the agency.

When we composed ourselves, I asked, "How, did this happen? You have been searching all these years. Your mother, father, sister?"

Sobbing. "Yes, they are all alive—Phyllis, can you believe?"

"Where are they?"

"In Gomel," she replies. "Do you remember Mrs. Sokolov, who comes into the office and sends packages to her relatives in Russia? She is such a nice lady. I wrote a visa for her to visit her brother in Belarus. I gave her the name of my family and I asked if she could please ask about them. You won't believe this, but she asked her brother and he had heard about them and they went and visited them and they are all alive. She came into the agency today and told me—I almost had a heart attack. I can't believe it…all these eighteen years I didn't know whether they were dead or alive. Everyone who went to Russia, I would beg them to look and no one could tell me anything. I can't believe… that she found my family, my mother, father, my sister Riva. I have to go lie down a moment. I just can't believe it."

My mother threw herself into the complicated process of obtaining a visa to see her family, made more difficult by the fact that she had left Russia as a Soviet citizen and was now requesting special permission to stay with her parents in Gomel, something the USSR rarely granted. She finally received clearance to travel in 1964.

When she returned to the United States she was visibly distraught about her family and their living conditions. Worrying about them now took the place of lamenting having lost them.

My mother's visit stimulated my desire to meet my grandparents. Since I was majoring in Russian literature and politics, the idea occurred to me to spend my junior year abroad in Russia, but my mother actively discouraged me from studying in the USSR, having witnessed the grim atmosphere of the country and the difficult living conditions. Instead I decided to travel to Russia the following summer.

But my trip was not to be. Tragedy intervened with my father's sudden death from a massive heart attack at the age of fifty in December of 1964. My mother, just reunited with her family, had now lost her husband and I, having recently acquired grandparents, now suffered the unbearable loss of my beloved father.

I forced myself to complete my midyear finals, but for the remainder of my junior year I just went through the motions of studying, in shock at my father's sudden death. I worried about my mother living alone and wanted to be back home in Chicago.

As luck would have it, the University of Illinois was building a second campus on the west side of Chicago. Nevertheless, because my mother had settled into her life alone and it was no longer so easy at home, when I graduated in 1966 I left for a four-month tour of Europe that included visiting Russia. Because Gomel was not on the approved list for foreign visitors, my mother advised me to visit the approved cities in the Soviet Union. She suggested I could save time if I applied for a visa in Paris, my first European destination. My grandparents could meet me in Leningrad.

Once in Paris, I naively struck on the idea of requesting a visa to journey by train from Paris to Russia by way of Germany and Poland rather than flying from Paris to Moscow. I wanted to see the country where my father was born and raised.

I presented myself to the travel authorities in Paris. I was told to leave my passport and return in a few days. The few days stretched into weeks with no visa in sight. Unexpectedly alone in Paris, I was filled with second thoughts about the ambitious and solitary journey I had undertaken to reunite with my grandparents.

I have a vivid memory of crossing the Pont Notre-Dame, lonely and homesick, looking up through tear-filled eyes and seeing the cathedral appear before me bathed in golden light, a scene familiar from all the impressionist paintings. Gazing at the beauty of Notre-Dame, the play of lights on the Seine, the boats cruising down the river, the Parisians walking along the streets and over the bridges, like many before and after me I fell helplessly in love with Paris. I willed myself to stop crying and bless my good fortune at being detained in this city. On that very day I bought a chic new black bathing suit that I planned to wear on the Black Sea in Yalta.

I stayed in a hotel on the attic floor on Rue Du Sommerard, in the Latin Quarter. When I was not walking I sat in cafes writing letters home about my enchantment with the city. Before I left for Paris, my mother's best friend Paula had given me an introduction to her cousin who had a son my age graduating from the Polytechnique. I waited awhile to call her and she invited me to dinner. Her son asked me to go along with him and his friends on a car rally scavenger hunt as part of the graduation events. I had no idea what was involved. Driving through the French countryside I was transfixed as we followed the tricky clues leading from one unusual or beautiful destination to another. One clue in particular was difficult to work out because it was a special tree located in the woods. I pictured myself in a French movie as we ran in different directions through the woods searching for this one tree. Finding the next clue tucked in the bark of the tree, we stopped to have a picnic lunch and relax. The last destination was an elegant multi-course dinner in a grand chateau.

The remainder of the time in Paris I walked non-stop as if in a dream. I was no longer homesick.

Eventually, I forced myself to return to the visa office and was informed that I could only obtain a visa to Russia by taking a flight to Moscow. I was incredulous. Why had they not told me this before? The man behind the desk explained that my passport stated I was born in Poland, and the Polish government had decreed that anyone who had left the country was not allowed to return. I was not allowed to cross Poland by train. He returned my passport and suggested I see a travel agent and purchase an airline ticket.

I had thought nothing of the fact that my passport read "*Place of Birth: Poland.*" I was sixteen years old when my mother told me I was born in Russia, not Poland, followed by, "You don't tell anyone. Ever!" This news was not startling, since there was never much conviction in her voice whenever she had to state where I was born. I never questioned her. From early on I understood that basic identifying information taken for granted by most people could not be taken for granted among refugees. Where someone had been born, lived, and spent the war years was often ambiguous and confusing. Was their name their original name or had it been changed? Was someone's spouse really Jewish or did they just say they were? Family members often teasingly questioned if my own mother was Jewish, with her green eyes, light hair, upturned nose and scanty knowledge of Jewish customs and the Yiddish language. Since I do not possess a birth certificate I never, to this day, feel certain of my age, the country of my birth or my original given name. After a lifetime in America when someone asks me where I was born, I still hear my mother's warning in my head and I hesitate, as if I might be in trouble, possibly deported. I am not certain to this day why my place of birth was changed. Our papers were drawn in Germany after escaping from Poland.

Perhaps the emigration laws and policies at that time forced people to 'adjust' identifying information. Perhaps my mother, still fearing the possibility of repercussions, waited to tell me about my actual birthplace until she was certain that I could keep this information secret. In 1966, when I was twenty-one years old, I was experiencing the return of the repressed as

I attempted to get a visa to travel to Russia. This "falsification" of my place of birth would continue to plague me on this trip in ways I had never imagined.

After leaving the visa office in Paris I walked into a travel agency and told the agent that I wanted to fly to Russia. Several days later I returned and the agent handed me Aeroflot tickets, a visa, my itinerary: Moscow-Leningrad-Yalta, as well as a pre-paid coupons for hotels and restaurants. As I left the agency, I imagined myself in the plane flying over Poland, looking down on the country I'm not allowed to enter and thinking to myself *perhaps some other time.*

As the jumbo Aeroflot plane is preparing for final descent I think: Am I really returning to 'Mother Russia,' the place of my birth where I will finally meet my grandparents? I'm experiencing a sense of unreality about the realm I am now entering. What is it going to be like to meet the people who are my closest blood relations, whom I don't know and who don't know me? My grandparents, aunt, relatives are known to me only through my mother's stories of loss, sadness, and tears. Will we be able to communicate in our foreign tongues? Will we understand one another coming from such different worlds? Will we have anything in common other than our family relationship? Our countries do not have warm relations. How will I be treated as an American?

My mother's preoccupation with her loss had been the fabric of our lives from the time she left Russia. Her visible states of unhappiness always associated in my mind with her lament about being "an orphan." Her mourning has been transmitted to me making me apprehensive about meeting my relatives. The obfuscation about the place of my birth had left me with a sense of confusion, and I longed to locate myself in time and place, so that when people asked, "Where do you come from?" I would not hesitate or deflect the question. In a couple of months, I would turn twenty-two, approximately the age of my mother when she left Russia. All the questions about my mother that had made her seem so different from my father and his family, questions that have preoccupied me through all my growing up, have led to make this inexplicable and solitary journey to meet the people called my grandparents. I felt anxious, yet immensely excited.

The plane lands smoothly on the runway. I disembark wearing a sleeveless, brown-and-white checked cotton mini-dress. At the baggage claim I spot my two oversized, heavy, canvas suitcases, grab their leather handles and proceed to drag them to customs inspection. The cases are filled with clothing my mother packed for her family; merchandise to sell on the black market where a couple of coats and shoes makes it possible for a family to buy food for a year. Goods brought into the country are heavily taxed, and visiting relatives declare the clothing for personal use. If the customs officer should decide to tax the contents, a tourist could choose to leave the merchandise with customs. Needless to say, the customs officials did quite well under this arrangement. As an Eastern European-In-Tourist Travel specialist, my mother chose the goods I brought to Russia for our relatives to either keep for personal use or sell.

I watch nervously as the customs inspector opens my suitcases. Among the items are three fake fur coats, an assortment of shoes, undergarments, nylon hosiery, dresses, and skirts. The garments are sized extra-large since Russian women are known to have substantial figures. There is an assortment of inexpensive cosmetics; lipsticks, rouge, mascara and nail polish, enough to fill a deep drawer. I had added several pairs of Levi jeans, chewing gum and perfume. The nylons and chewing gum will come in handy to give as tips in the hotels where I am booked. I watch the inspector pick up one of the oversized, brown fake fur coats, *Eto vashe? Is this yours?* I try very hard to show no facial expression and calmly say *eto moe. Its mine,* as my mother had instructed. We look at each other as if in a stand-off. He is a nice-looking middle-aged man with a pleasant face and calm demeanor. Still holding the coat in his hands and lightly stroking the fake fur, he looks me over carefully, taking note of my small frame. A skeptical expression appears on his face, and in a polite manner he asks, why I need such a heavy coat in May. I'm beginning to sweat, as if I were actually wearing the coat. Struggling with my poor conversational Russian, I reply, *Mne legko prostudit'sya,* I easily get cold. I'm trying my best to maintain a cool composure because the temptation to burst out laughing is overpowering. Observing myself in this interchange, I can't believe how bold I'm being. His eyes look amused, clearly trying not to smile, playing with me while trying to look serious. He takes a cursory look through the second suitcase, inspects the contents of my shoulder bag and motions for me to put everything back in the cases. With a wave of his hand he directs me through the custom aisle. I breathe a heavy sigh of relief, quickly make my way to the exit. Thinking about his kindness now, I imagine that he was surprised and touched by this young woman, still seemingly a girl, travelling alone from the far away land of America to see her *babushka* and *dedushka* in the Soviet Union.

I soon feel alone and despondent, an unusual specimen on these Soviet shores. My youthful enthusiasm, idealism and American optimism are clashing head on with the stark and oppressive reality of the USSR. The next day I receive a telegram from my aunt Riva that my grandfather is too ill to travel; therefore he and my grandmother, who does not want to leave his side, will not be meeting me in Leningrad. Only Riva will come. I feel utterly crushed by this news. Not to see them! This can't be, I must get to Gomel! A rush of adrenaline has me on my feet running to find some Russian authority in charge, determined to make a case for being allowed to travel to see them.

I show the person in charge of foreign visitors at the hotel the telegram and plead my case to grant me a special visa. Unsympathetic, he tells me in a cold, officious manner, *nevozmozhno,* Not possible. He adds what I already know, that I have no choice but to follow the iron clad itinerary: Moscow-Leningrad-Yalta. My transportation, hotels and meals were pre-paid in Paris and exchanged for a book of coupons for the remainder of my stay. Tourists are only allowed to stay in places where the Soviet authorities can keep a watchful eye on all their comings and goings. Thus, I will stay in 'approved hotels,' with a matron stationed on all the floors to keep watch. The government is not eager for foreigners, particularly Americans, to mingle freely with their citizens and certainly not with their Russian relatives who do not have an approved hotel in Gomel.

Yet ordinary Russian citizens show immense curiosity and hunger for any news of the outside world. In Moscow, people follow me on the street, in art museums, eager to speak to an American. I have an odd sensation that they want to physically touch me to see if I am real. I'm also stopped and asked for American cigarettes, chewing gum or something to sell, such as a watch or jeans. All these restrictions are incomprehensible to my American mind and as the days of my visit pass, I struggle with disturbing thoughts and emotions. I'm not prepared for the feeling of surveillance and suspicion that I encounter and slowly it dawns on me that the state of paranoia I feel is perhaps an adaptive response to a malignant environment.

The plane touches down in Leningrad. I make my way to the baggage claim, pick up my luggage and then proceed to locate the car waiting to take me to the hotel. After checking in and handing over a number of coupons to the receptionist, a hotel worker helps with my luggage and shows me to my room. I take a quick glance around the small room and see that it is clean, basic and nondescript. I hastily wash up in the bathroom that sports a large white tub, take the elevator back to the lobby, anxious to see Riva. But I haven't shaken the despondent feeling of the news that my grandparents will not be traveling to Leningrad. The excitement I first felt upon arrival in Russia has been replaced by disappointment and weariness, a weariness that comes with feeling powerless in the face of the Soviet's immovable stance in granting me the visa to Gomel.

As the elevator doors open, my eyes are drawn to a short, heavy woman standing nearby with a worried expression on her face. She appears to be searching for someone. From the photographs my mother brought back from her visit to Russia in 1964, I slowly recognize the woman as my aunt Riva. Standing beside her is a man wearing a camel hair double-breasted coat. She catches my gaze, stares at me, and in disbelief her pale gray eyes look into my incredulous stare. A painful cry emerges from the depth of her body and in a deep voice she says, "*Filiss?*" Tears flowing, she embraces me. I'm also crying as my arms surround her, a woman who is a stranger to me yet uncannily familiar. When we let go of one another, I look at her more closely, notice her thinning brown hair and prominent breasts that emphasize her full body. She wears a knee length shift, exposing two thin legs in high heels that look incongruous with the body weight they support. I recognize the blue printed material of the dress my mother sent to her overseas. I feel some shame at thinking her unattractive and can't help comparing her with my beautiful, glamorous mother.

Her companion is standing to the side, as if not wanting to intrude on our reunion. He is a stocky man with a broad chest and a pleasant round open face. He offers his hand and I feel the warmth of his greeting as he calls me the affectionate name of *Felichka*. Riva says, *Eto Senya, nasha sosed*—this is Senya, our neighbor. I will meet Senya agian, an artist and illustrator, when he and his wife emigrate to New York in the nineteen-eighties. He will give me several drawings of my family, including a tempera drawing of my grandparents in front of their house in Gomel in 1932.

I suggest that we go to the room but they seem to hesitate, looking at each other, turning their heads as they scan the lobby, nodding and then cautiously following me into the elevator. Once in the room Riva, in a rush of words, repeats what I already know, my grandparents are not coming. Neither Riva nor Senya speak English, and I'm struggling to comprehend her Russian. I press her for details of my grandfather's illness. She does not reply, and i I see her eyes scanning the sparse room. She finally says; *Poydem, my pokazhem vam vokrug goroda*—let's go, we will show you around the city and she quickly moves towards the door.

Later I will come to learn that while my relatives are eager to hear about my life in America, they will not engage in such conversations in hotel rooms, restaurants, or certain public places. When we are in my hotel room they look for planted surveillance devices. When in a restaurant they look around to make sure that no one is overhearing our conversation. In order to feel on safe ground, we walk arm in arm in different parks (a favorite pastime of many citizens) and stop to sit on benches where I ask them questions about their life in Russia and describe my life in the States.

Riva will accompany me for the remainder of my stay in Russia and there will be times when I will be very frustrated by her. Her habit of never offering an opinion, even on what seems to me to be the smallest of matters, will make me impatient with her. When I ask her what she would like to eat, she never directly answers and instead shrugs, almost always deferring to me.

It will be more than twenty years later, in the eighties, with the wave of new Russian immigrants coming to the States, that I will look back and better understand my aunt's psychology and her reluctance to openly say what she thought or felt. In the Soviet Union what was not provided by the government was often procured by manipulating the system or bartered on the black market. Housing, medical care, and education are provided by the State but the living conditions for the average citizen, apart from the higher party officials, are poor. An extended family typically lives in two rooms with a shared kitchen and bath. Long lines for food and merchandise are everywhere and food is rationed. Families are placed on waiting lists for years to get separate apartments, refrigerators or stoves. Married couples have little choice but to live with their parents in over-crowded quarters. The system breeds mistrust, including mistrust towards one's neighbors.

I assume that Riva's reluctance to express any opinion or desire was a result of a life long need to be very careful about what she said and who might hear. For example, when the family received a package from my mother, they no doubt would slip it into their home to avoid their neighbors' curious eyes. Fearing exposure and covering feelings, thoughts and opinions can lead to a general suppression of desire, producing a state of mind that can ultimately lead to not being able recognize what one wants. When supplies are rare, a person's dreams and hopes can become a disappointment. I wonder if Riva may have reached that state of mind -where no desires were openly expressed beyond what was immediate and practical—and thus she had become the wary, uncomplicated person I came to know. Even asking her what she would like to eat was more than her mind dare imagine or maybe hope for. I think if I had simply asked her if she was hungry and wanted to eat, she would have answered "yes."

And yet Riva and Senya were able to enjoy the available and affordable pleasures. They proudly showed me all the sights in Leningrad, a city that offers much enchantment.

We stroll arm in arm after midnight on Nevsky Prospekt, the main street of the city, transfixed by the "White Nights" that occur from May to July, when the city celebrates nearly round-the clock daylight and when the sky is one long sunset of amber, red, and violet. Unlike Moscow with its inhuman scale buildings and drab atmosphere, Leningrad is a beautiful, regal looking city, and there is a greater sense of enjoyment of daily life compared to Moscow. Recently emerged from the cold and dark of winter, the wide avenue of Nevsky Prospekt is filled with people promenading, their heavy winter garments shed, enjoying the evening air, eating ice cream, talking and looking unusually relaxed. Senya, a frequent visitor to the famous Hermitage museum, becomes our tour guide. I am stunned by the grandeur of this former Winter Palace of the czars and its vast holdings. Senya describes the storerooms below ground, immense as the building itself and holding incalculable numbers of paintings never shown. Only a fraction of the art is visible to the public because the art restorers, with little money available, can't keep up with the demand for restoration.

We leave the museum and walk along the beautiful Neva River that snakes through the city cutting it in half. The following night we will go to the Marinsky Theater to see the Kirov Ballet, a dream come true for me as my mother often spoke of the Bolshoi and Kirov Ballet companies. I find myself thinking of my mother in this city where her university education was interrupted by the war, and remember how excited she became when she took me to see performances of the famous ballet companies that toured Chicago.

On our last day we visit Peterhof Fountains and Gardens. The fountains were a part of Peter the Great's grand plan for Peterhof Palace which is called the "Russian Versailles." Senya takes many photos of us in front of these spectacular fountains spouting their spray high in the air.

That evening we are invited to dinner at Senya's apartment in Leningrad to meet his son, a magician, and his young grandson. My mother's cousin Alex, has come from Simfiropol to meet me. Before we arrive at Senya's apartment we stop in a bakery to buy a chocolate cake. I'm astounded at the price of the cake. Alex insists on paying for it and I'm feeling very guilty about what they will have to deny themselves to honor me with this cake.

The next morning, we visit the In-Tourist shop for foreign tourists that carries goods not available in the department stores or markets, such as electronics, clothing, watches, specialty foods and Russian souvenirs. Riva declines everything but I insist on purchasing some items for Alex and her. Later I suspect that Alex was eager that I take him to this store for some gifts. I recall little of the flight from Leningrad, other than feeling very sad that I had to follow the "prescribed route" to Yalta, losing all hope of seeing my grandparents.

Ten days later, Moscow and Leningrad are now behind me. I am lying face down on a crowded beach on the Black Sea in Yalta. The pebbly sand under my body is gray and rough and I feel weary, disheartened and hopeless. I'm thinking about what to do next when my attention is suddenly drawn to hushed Russian voices above me. Startled and confused, as if waking from a dream, I slowly raise my head and see a group of men and women, many quite stout and wearing poorly fitting bathing suits surrounding me and pointing at my body. As the kaleidoscopic vision comes into focus, I gradually comprehend what is happening. They are transfixed, pointing at the black bathing suit I purchased in Paris. The suit's top is attached to the bottom half by two identical large silver rings on the front and back, giving the impression of two tips of a triangle held together by the ring in the center of my abdomen. This swimsuit would be certain to turn eyes in the States, but here on the Black Sea in May of 1966, wearing such a fashionable suit is enough to make me look like someone who has just landed from an alien planet. Even apart from this dramatic costume, I am looked upon as that unusual specimen: a twenty-one -year-old female alone in a country where people see few foreigners. I'm a bit embarrassed by the stir my Parisian bathing suit has caused and decide to return to the hotel.

As I walk along the beach towards the hotel I notice a ramshackle one-room structure that serves as the local police station. On impulse I walk in, deciding to make one last desperate attempt to plead with the official in charge for permission to see my grandparents in Gomel.

The police officer in the station seems different from the bureaucratic officials I encountered in Moscow and Leningrad, kinder and more sympathetic. I'm certain that not many young American women suddenly show up in his small station on the beach. In my poor conversational Russian, with tears in my eyes I tell him of my journey from America to Russia, of my attempts to visit the grandparents I've yet to meet. All my frustrations come pouring out as I speak of my grandfather who is ill, of my grandmother who won't leave his side, of all my requests for permission for a short visit denied.

My story appears to move him, and like others I've encountered, he's amazed by my traveling alone. He peppers me with questions about America based on what he's read in Russian newspapers or seen on television; our role in Vietnam, the Kennedy assassination, the Civil Rights marches, drugs, Chicago gangsters. I explain there are no longer Chicago gangsters with machine guns killing people as depicted in American films, but I can't contradict the images on Russian television depicting our Civil Rights struggle or justify why we are in Vietnam.

Like other Russians, he is visibly hungry for any news that I can offer from the outside world. Meeting me is a rare opportunity to speak to someone from the country that plays such an overriding role in the ideology and foreign policies of his government. I sense in him a familiar quality of character reminiscent of my parents' close circle of refugee friends—his Slavic emotionality, warmth and interest in me. He says he will try to help me but can't guarantee that he will be successful. He asks the name of my hotel, tells me that I should wait and he will be in contact. I leave feeling not altogether hopeful but his seemingly genuine interest leaves me feeling a bit better.

The sun is blaring down on me. I still feel emotional, hot and fatigued and decide to stop at one of the beach concessions to cool off with some ice cream. I find a seat and pass time watching the Soviet citizens enjoy their day at the beach; sunbathing, walking along the shore, looking for small treasures in the sand, standing and socializing in the shallow water, keeping cool. I'm still thinking about my encounter with the policeman, aware of reawakened stirrings of hope. Then I slowly head back to the hotel. As I approach, I see my Aunt Riva running towards me in her blue shift dress, breathing heavily and looking distraught. Her looks again take me aback; she doesn't in the least resemble my petite, green-eyed, blond-haired mother.

Shouting something that I can't understand, she stops in front of me, catches her breath, and in a rush of words tells me that the police came looking for me at the hotel, then adds, "What could they want, what have you done?" She looks terrified as I try to reassure her that this might indeed be good news. I turn around and very excited, head back to the police station leaving Riva no choice but to run breathlessly after me.

We sit at a desk in the station facing the policeman who tells me that I have permission for a three-day visit to my grandparents, hands me a visa, and tells me to go and purchase plane tickets. I can't believe my ears and burst out crying. I'm often crying these days and attribute my volatile emotional state to trying to contain the frustration and anxiety that has become an ever-present traveling companion. I look over at Riva sitting next to me and see the look of confusion and disbelief on her face as she looks at me, then back to the man behind the desk. I can't find words to thank this person who has given me this unbelievable gift. As we leave the station my aunt grabs my arm and says, *malodetz,* a name for someone who has accomplished an extraordinary feat. She lets go of my arm and runs ahead to send a telegram to my grandparents: *We are coming to Gomel!* I take off in the other direction to find a travel office to book a flight for Riva and myself.

The rude travel agent in a forceful tone categorically announces that there are no flights to Gomel, and dismisses me as if to say "end of subject." I stand my ground, argue that this is impossible since my mother flew to Gomel two years ago. Grudgingly, she picks up a piece of paper listing plane schedules, looks at it and tells me that I can get to Gomel, but that I have to change planes in Minsk. Again, I am incredulous at this manner of doing business. She warns me that there is a very brief window of time in Minsk to transfer planes to Gomel and looks at me as if to say, "Don't blame me if you don't make the connection," with I told you so, in her voice. I answer, "I will take my chances, I want the tickets, please." Begrudgingly, she completes my purchase and hands over the tickets to my grandparents' home.

The next day my aunt and I leave Yalta and a few hours later we land in Minsk. As we disembark from the plane and hurriedly walk down the steps, determined to catch our flight to Gomel, I hear my name being called. A young man with blond hair, about my age, wearing a grey suit and tie, a blank expression on his face, says in a serious voice, "Please come with me." His eyes turn to Riva, "Please come along." In a frantic tone I try to ask him what this is all about, and pointing to a small plane nearby I try to explain that we need to catch another flight, we have very little time before the plane leaves. His face shows no expression and he repeats that I must come with him. I hear the voice of the agent in my head saying, *I told you so*. Riva follows behind visibly distressed. A car is waiting for us and we are told to get in. After a short distance the car comes to a stop in front of a typical imposing Russian government building. We get out of the car, are ushered into the building through the large entrance, up a staircase, down a long hallway lined with many identical doors. We are stopped in front of one of them.

The room we enter is large and bare apart from a huge wooden desk that dominates the space. An attractive, imposing looking man dressed in a gray suit, white shirt, and tie, sits behind the desk looking down at some papers. He raises his head and with a noncommittal gaze looks at us, gestures for us to sit down on two hard, wooden chairs stationed across the desk from him. He introduces himself as the head of the police in Minsk and asks us to explain what we are doing here in Minsk. I repeat my story, that I have come to see my grandparents in Gomel and that a police officer in Yalta gave me permission to travel and arranged for a three- day visa. In a very cold manner he points out that I was given this visa in the Ukraine and I am now in Belarus and therefore the visa is not valid. I am struggling with my limited Russian, but suddenly remember how to say "regional," and so I proceed to say something about how I don't understand their regional problems, only that I was given a visa to travel to Gomel. He is looking at my passport and asks me where I was born. Just as I am about to say Poland, my aunt interrupts and begins to say Russia. I quickly speak over her before she says another word and hope he hasn't heard her. It suddenly occurs to me that my aunt has no knowledge of my parents changing the place of my birth. For the first time during the course of this trip I am afraid and wonder if perhaps I have gone too far in my determination to see my grandparents. In a stern voice the head of police states we are to spend the night in Minsk; they will let me know of their decision the next morning. In the meantime, I should use my coupons to pay for the hotel where I will be staying.

Once again, I have no idea what will happen next. Added to the possibility of not being allowed to travel to Gomel, will I even be allowed to leave Russia? Could I possibly be shipped to the Gulag? I try to put these dark thoughts out of my mind. I realize I have not eaten in a long time and I'm hungry. My poor aunt at this point is white as a sheet. To distract ourselves from our growing fear, I suggest we eat and afterwards go to a movie. But the movie playing in a theater near the hotel does not put my mind to rest, quite the contrary. In this oversized movie theater, packed with Russians, I am probably the only foreigner and surely the only American. Before the main attraction begins, a newsreel is shown of the recent May Day Parade, taking place in Moscow's Red Square. On the screen in front of my disbelieving eyes, I watch a parade of trucks carrying missiles, huge tanks, machine guns, and an assortment of armaments. Following behind this spectacle of weapons of destruction are thousands of Russian uniformed soldiers marching in unison, carrying firearms, accompanied by thunderous marching bands playing patriotic music. There is no subtlety in the footage of this film; the aim is to demonstrate Russia's supreme power. Given my state of mind, current circumstance, and my youth, the film only intensifies my fear that has been growing since we landed in Minsk.

The propaganda assault on all my senses ceases and the main attraction begins. While the May Day parade is to show the dominance of the Soviet Union as a superpower, the movie I now watch depicts the humble, proud, young working-class Russian laborers: industrious, yet fun-loving, sentimental, and romantic. The movie is a silly caricature of a romance between two young bright eyed, good natured, healthy looking young people happily working on a *kolhoz*, the famous "collective farm." These young comrades are shown joyfully working in the fields, bound together for the common good and love of the Soviet Union. At night they get together, sing, flirt, and have their moments of their romance and heartbreak. To my Western eye, the film looks poorly made and acted, definitely inferior to American and French cinema. This is pure propaganda. It makes me sad to think that the same country that I so admire for its great filmmaker Eisenstein and its literary geniuses such as Tolstoy, Pushkin, Dostoyevsky, and Chekhov has come to this. But for the moment, seeing the movie and reflecting on what Communism has wrought has distracted me from worries about my current situation.

Utterly exhausted, Riva and I return to our hotel, get into bed, anxious and not knowing what tomorrow will bring. In the morning we arise early, quickly dress and hurry back to keep our appointment with the head of police. Once again, we are shown into the room where we were detained the day before. This morning the official looks friendlier and less forbidding. In a direct manner he tells us we have permission to continue on to Gomel and hands back my passport and visa. I start shaking with relief. I thank him profusely and we quickly leave. The young man who met me and angered me because he would not let us catch our plane for Gomel accompanies us back to the airport. As I am boarding the steps to the plane I notice he is holding an apple in his hand and offers it to me, clearly a peace offering for having been so cold and rude when we met the first time. I'm very touched and take the apple. I smile say *spaciba*, and shake his hand good by. My mind goes to the movie we saw the previous night about the romance between two young people on the *kolhoz*. Over and over I'm struck by the paradoxical nature of the Russian people I encounter. Alongside the cruelty, suspicion, self-centeredness, coldness and rudeness, I also see and feel their passionate, empathic, kind, generous and sentimental side. Both feel real.

Riva and I have just boarded a decrepit looking propeller aircraft. Two long wooden benches face one another instead of the individual passenger seats to which I am accustomed. Could the plane be a holdover from World War II? More likely it reflects the general shortage of material goods that are common in this country. There are about twenty very solemn looking passengers in the act of investigating long straps they hold in their hands, attached to the back of the benches. I look for mine, feeling slightly relieved that we each have our own individual seatbelts. The stewardess in a loud, officious, impatient voice, as if speaking to inattentive school children, instructs the passengers on how to buckle our belts. I'm not a comfortable air traveler in general, and this aircraft does little to ease my increasing anxiety. The engines labor as the airplane finally lifts into the wide expanse of the clear sky. I begin to relax as we fly smoothly over the desolate countryside below.

I think of the kindness of the customs official, the policemen in Yalta and in Minsk, and the young man who offered me an apple, and wonder what has allowed these men to break with the official Soviet policy. Could it be their admiration and wonder in meeting a young American woman travelling alone? Identifying with my desire to pursue a reunion with lost relatives? No doubt they themselves must have been separated from or lost loved ones. But I suspect there might be other reasons involved in bending the rules. I wonder if perhaps I represented a breath of fresh air, a young American women of the 60s generation, enjoying the freedom they would have liked, in contrast to their restricted lives in a country that rarely allows citizens to travel. By my action of challenging the Soviet travel policy and their coming to my aid, they briefly defied the limitation on their lives, sharing my independence and autonomy.

Surrounded by the deafening noise of the engines, my mind turns to what it will be like to see my grandparents. As I conjure up a vision of the reunion, I am suddenly distracted by a figure emerging from the cockpit. The pilot, smiling, stops in front of me, shakes my hand and greets me with *Amerikanska*! All the other passengers liven up and are staring at me. I'm straining to have a polite conversation, while at the same time my mind is preoccupied with the thought of who is flying the plane. The pilot is making small talk and I'm appropriately nodding and smiling in response, as if I understand and agree with everything he is saying. Suddenly there is some unexpected turbulence and the pilot quickly returns to his cabin. Once more I'm struck by the eagerness of the people to be in contact and to communicate with an American, and I envision the pilot going home to his family and friends, bringing news about the young woman on his flight from Minsk to Gomel.

A young girl sitting directly across from me is obviously airsick and begins to vomit into the clear plastic bag given to us for this purpose. I try to avert my eyes from the bag and find myself once more astonished by what I see in this country as making little common sense. So much is dysfunctional, the airsickness bag being a case in point. No apparent thought or care has gone into providing a bag that is not transparent. Could it be that things that appear crude and cruel to someone coming from the West have little importance in this country? Or perhaps the Russians have come to expect very little since resources are scarce, unlike in America where the abundance of goods and choices are taken for granted?

The pilot announces that we are landing and immediately the plane begins its quick descent, abruptly touches down and bumps to a stop. We all sit quietly waiting for instructions as a stepladder materializes and is dropped from the floor of the plane. While the other passengers are collecting their belongings and head towards the exit, the stewardess asks Riva and me to wait until the others disembark. I am a foreigner on Russian soil; here again I'm closely watched. Finally, I see a nod from the stewardess granting permission for us to leave the plane.

From the plane's doorway, I look out at a crystal blue sky above and an expansive grass field below where the plane landed. Moving towards us in the distance are two figures, like dots on the landscape. Riva excitedly tells me that it must be "babushka" and her cousin Natasha. The scene has an unreal quality like the frame of a film, and I feel eerily strange and dissociated as I walk toward the shapes. The figures are moving closer and as they slowly come into focus. I see two women walking briskly with large bouquets of wild flowers gathered in their arms. A compact elderly woman with bright blue eyes that match the sky, silver grey hair braided atop of her head, wearing a loose flowered shift, reaches me, embraces me, and in that moment I find myself overcome with a well of suppressed emotion. In her embrace I feel my mother's tears, all the absences and all the losses. But in that embrace, I also feel the fulfillment of all that has been elusive, disjointed and confusing about my roots. I feel more arms enfolding me, women hugging me, crying, touching my face, as if in disbelief that I'm real. We are reunited here in Russia. I have returned to the place of my origin.

Twenty years had passed since my parents and I left Russia. During those years I shared my mother's longings and hopes to find her parents, my grandparents. My mother is now forty-four, and in two months I will be twenty-two, the age she was when she gave birth to me. Having arrived at the threshold of my grandparent's home, will I finally have answers to the many questions that remain a mystery? Will I have the satisfaction of completing the puzzle of my origins? Here in Gomel where she was born and raised, will I learn more about my complicated mother? I have been thrown an anchor, but can I grasp hold of it while I am swimming in a turbulent sea of emotions? This tumultuous journey trying to reach Gomel has left me overexcited, overwhelmed, depleted and utterly exhausted.

The house before me is not my mother's childhood home, nor the one in the tempera drawing that Senya drew depicting my grandparents sitting relaxed in chairs placed in the front yard. That home was evacuated when the Germans entered Gomel and was confiscated during the war by the Soviet authorities and this current house was assigned upon their return from Ulyanovsk. It is one among many similar houses situated on a narrow road, its surroundings giving the appearance of a rural village. The location is particularly surprising because I will later discover that the center of the city of Gomel is a short distance away. The house is mostly hidden from view by a tall rustic, gray, wooden fence; I look up to see a pitched roof with two chimneys. Behind the fence stands a small stucco building with an entrance door and two small windows on opposite sides of the door opening into a dimly lit entrance hall. I enter the space, adjusting my sight to the gray light, my eyes slowly coming to rest on a dilapidated stove covered with soot. The entrance must also serve as the kitchen. I notice a woman standing in a doorway. Riva looks obliged to introduce us before she takes my elbow and hurriedly nudges me through a second door. The neighbor, while curious to meet the American relative, has no chance to become acquainted. It is apparent from Riva's impolite introduction she is not eager for me to interact with her. I later learn that two separate families live in one room of this two-room dwelling with its shared kitchen.

As I am ushered into my grandparents living quarters, a tall, frail man with a bald head and oval shaped face moves towards me. His deeply lined face and sad eyes have the look of a man who has endured much hardship, yet something of his bearing suggests that at one time he was a handsome, imposing figure. My grandfather takes both my hands into his, takes a step back, examines me as if in wonder and meets my gaze. My own eyes fill with tears as he takes me in his arms. Everyone is now standing around us crying… Grandmother, Riva, Natasha.

Riva pulls herself away from our circle, wipes her tears, takes charge and says *sidyts*—come sit. The spacious room serves as the living room and bedroom. A table in the center is the gathering area for the family. She orders Natasha to help with the suitcases left by the door and leads me to the table. As is the custom for special celebrations, the table is covered in a white linen tablecloth with a pale green border and matching woven napkins. *Zakuski*, appetizers, cover the entire table, leaving the white cloth beneath barely visible. I experience a rush of nostalgic memories of the favorite foods served at home with my family. The *zakuski* include potatoes, mushrooms, eggs, and beet salads, pickled herring, *perogi* (meat filled dumplings), stuffed cabbage, *kotleti* (small hamburgers) and fish accompanied by a great deal of sour cream and of course a bottle of vodka. I am taken aback at the quantity and variety of food. I take little bites but feel too emotional to swallow. I am trying to follow the excited conversation of Riva explaining how it was that we were given permission to travel to Gomel. And once again I keep hearing her repeat *ona molodetz,* she is brave. My grandparents and Natasha are listening, shaking their heads, looking at me in disbelief and repeating *ne mogu eto poverit*, it's unbelievable. Riva, in an excited voice describes our adventure with the police in Minsk, interrupted by questions and exclamations.

While Riva is talking, my eyes once more focus on all the food in front of me. They have gone to a great deal of trouble and cost to include some of the delicacies that undoubtedly were purchased on the black market. Suddenly Riva stands up and begins to clear the table of the remaining *zakuski*. I feel relief that the meal is coming to an end. But no, the main dishes are now served—*borcht*, a beet soup followed by chicken Kiev.

For the third time the table is cleared and an assortment of desserts and sweets appear along with Russian *chai*. While we are drinking our tea, my grandfather slowly gets up and comes back to the table with a Russian-English dictionary. I speak English along with my rudimentary Russian as we try to converse. My grandfather often turns to the dictionary for help with the English words, and I am impressed with how he perseveres despite his ill health.

Finally, the meal comes to an end. My grandfather excuses himself, saying he is tired and needs to rest. Riva and my grandmother are removing the remaining dishes from the table. I look around at the sparsely furnished but comfortable room. Two small beds rest against the opposite walls of the room, enclosed by curtains, obviously to offer some privacy. I smile when I see the famous Russian stove described with fondness by my mother, the stove that kept the tea in the samovar heated all day and held a special place for the cat to keep warm. I suspect the stove my mother recalled was larger than this one whose primary purpose is to heat the room. I am reminded of the gift of a samovar that my mother brought home from her visit. How disappointed I was to discover that it was an electrified samovar and not a real one.

A white-laced curtained window looks out onto a yard that serves as a kitchen garden where corn, potatoes, cabbage, and greens are grown. The garden reminds me of the lines in front of food stores in Moscow and Leningrad, lines that seemed infinite because little food was available and people waited for hours hoping they were not waiting in vain. I think about the cake Alex bought for our dinner at Senya's.

I try to make myself feel better with the thought that my grandparents can at least grow some of the food they need. But the feeling is short-lived and gives way to an overwhelming sense of guilt that my grandparents honored my visit with such an extravagant costly meal.

I ask Riva to show me to the bathroom, and to my surprise she takes my hand and leads me out into the yard along a path to an outhouse. Taken aback by the primitive living conditions, I return the next morning to the yard and take a Polaroid picture of the outhouse. In later years when I look at this photograph, I will experience guilt and embarrassment at the youthful insensitivity that led me to take the photo. Today I'm aware it was an emotional shock to witness the living conditions of my family. The photo was an attempt to distance myself from overwhelming feelings, acting the role of a tourist to convince myself that this "quaint outhouse" had no relation to me.

When I return from the outhouse, Riva, again in her take- charge voice, announces that we should all now go to sleep, as tomorrow will be a long day visiting Gomel and seeing more relatives. I welcome the idea of finally getting into bed. But where are we all going to sleep since there are only two beds? I can't imagine sharing this narrow bed with my aunt. As if reading my mind, Riva insists that I take her bed and that she will go stay with a friend. Once more the familiar feeling of guilt overcomes me at depriving Riva of her bed, but I am so exhausted that I simply thank her.

I can't sleep. Swirling through my mind are all the events of the day. It is beyond strange to be here in this room with my sleeping grandparents in another bed, grandparents I have not known until today. I think of my mother growing up in Gomel under these conditions although I know that this was not the home she grew up in. And yet her stories were not of hardship but of a carefree childhood. Could it be that her memories were romanticized to comfort her when she believed that her parents were no longer alive and that she was an orphan?

My grandmother had grown up in Lithuania in a family that was economically comfortable. Her maiden name was Stokolnytz, derived from the word glass, as the family had a glass making business. She had relatives who came to the United States in the early 1900's and established a glass factory in the Midwest where they turned out vases and other decorative items for the home. When we arrived in the US, I recall some of these same relatives giving us baroque gilded vases and candlesticks. During my childhood I was struck by how little my mother had to say about her own mother in contrast to her father. Her dim recollection was mysterious given her concerns about the loss of her parents. I sometimes insisted that she tell me something about her mother and she would say: "Mother was very beautiful and spoiled, and father gave in to her." Early on I suspected that my mother's outward independence and self-assurance hid her dependent longings to be admired, loved and cared for. Her relationship to her mother was not warm and nurturing, and that may be why I often felt that she saw me not only as her child but also as her wished for loving, good mother.

When she spoke about her father she always had a faraway look of longing in her eyes and told me that she was his favorite. Perhaps my mother's beauty and intelligence attracted the attention from my grandfather that was not available from my grandmother. During dinner when he painstakingly searched the dictionary for English words so that we could better understand each other, was he seeing his daughter in me?

His daughter, my mother, was a product of the Russian Revolution, born in 1922, five years after the Bolshevik Communist government led by Lenin came into power. Mother's voice was often filled with pride when she spoke of her father, an educated engineer by profession, and a highly respected card-carrying member of the Communist Party. It was particularly painful to her when she visited her parents in 1964, not having seen them for eighteen years, to discover that his standing in the Party had declined. She attributed this to anti-Semitism. With anger in her voice she told of an experience during the time of the visit: "There were some unpleasant things with the local authorities. I came into the house and my father was gone. Riva told me they called him in for questioning, probably wanting to know what he was telling me. I ran to the office where he was taken, yelling at them that they had no right to question him. They let him leave with me and return home." This episode must have recalled repeated experiences under Stalin and later during the war, when relatives, friends and neighbors were called in for questioning by the police, arrested or simply disappeared. I felt fear when I heard her encounter with the police, imagining losing my own mother being detained and not allowed to return to the States.

Her schooling was under Stalin, who was referred to as Dyeda Stalin (Father Stalin). I picture her as the girl in the Russian posters looking starry-eyed, wearing dark short skirts, white blouses and the scarlet kerchiefs of the Young Pioneers. Reminiscing about her childhood, she sometimes quoted in Russian the oath of the Young Pioneers:

I, Sonja... joining the ranks of the V. I. Lenin All-Union Pioneer Organization, in the presence of my comrades solemnly promise: to love and cherish my Motherland passionately, to live as the great Lenin bade us, as the Communist Party teaches us, as require the laws of the Young Pioneers of the Soviet Union.

My mother and her Russian refugee friends had temperaments that leaned towards the dramatic, sentimental, and nostalgic. They were strongly identified with their Russian origins and their early communist education. However, as immigrants in the US, it also became clear to them that the USSR was a totalitarian state, eventually leaving them with little love for Russia. My mother became a very proud and patriotic American, and political arguments between her and my father about the Soviet Union could become heated. My father maintained an idealistic picture of socialism, stemming from his own leftist leanings when he was a young man in Poland. My mother's work offered her a window into everyday life of the average citizen in the Soviet Union, and her disapproval of some of the actions of the newly arrived Soviet citizens, whom she viewed as products of a communist regime, contributed to her negative views on communist governments. She was an ardent supporter of democratic process, maintaining that it was an honor to be an American and to live in a free country.

Yet, she too held contradictory beliefs about Russia, in her nostalgia for her childhood. Years later, she and her friend Vera visited me in New York where I lived, and I took the opportunity to ask them some questions about their memories of life under Stalin. They did not speak of the brutalities of Stalin; instead they were in the thrall of reminiscence, looking back at the fun they enjoyed with their young comrades. Spontaneously they broke out in patriotic songs, and their voices rang out with a proud and youthful spirit that conveyed their idealism and hope for a new society. I asked if they remembered being afraid and was stunned by their seeming nonchalance as they recalled classmates whose fathers disappeared. It was as if their fond memories were dissociated from the terrifying happenings of the Stalin regime. Did they need to hold on to happy memories of their childhood in the face of all they lost? Did they have mixed feelings that came after the idealism that ushered in the revolution? Or was it a remnant of their Soviet indoctrination, lectured not to speak ill of the Russian government or its leaders? Ambiguous and contradictory feelings like this are not rare in people who ones joined in a common cause.

My mother attended the gymnasium and university in Leningrad until her studies were interrupted by the war. She had thoughts of becoming a doctor but decided to study literature. She described her childhood as uneventful, recalling the apples she picked from the trees in her back yard, playing with her cousins, walking in the woods, the taste of wild berries. She enjoyed cross-country skiing to school and told of her father making her first pair of skis. She also loved to ice skate. I was ten or eleven years old, living in Chicago, when she taught me how to skate on the school's frozen playground. I recall being very surprised (never having seen her on skates), how she put them on, stood up, clasped her hands behind her back and effortlessly glided across the ice. At that moment I saw my mother as a Sonja Henie; the famous ice skater, their shared first name only increased my admiration for her. When performances of the "Ice Capades" came to Chicago she made sure to take me to see them.

Among the few photos that she carried from Russia, there is a group photo of two young women and eight young men, most likely from when she first started university. They are sitting on a bench in the woods, one young man holding a guitar in his lap. Then I also recall the get-togethers my parents held in our room in the DP camp or later at home in Chicago, hearing my mother's lovely voice among the other voices, a friend playing a harmonica or accordion.

Her life as she knew it ended when the war began. Her words, often repeated, come back to me: "The war made a Jew of me." I have never taken this to mean she literally did not know she was Jewish, since she had some memories of her grandmother speaking Yiddish. But her family did not openly speak of being Jewish and, given that they were Communists, religion did not have a place in their lives. She knew little of Jewish history or traditions, and unlike my father and his family, she did not speak Yiddish. Growing up in Chicago, I even wondered if my mother was in fact Jewish, since she was also "teased" by my father's relatives that she was "passing as a Jew."

Lying in Riva's bed and thinking about the mother who grew up in Gomel, and the one I left behind in Chicago, I can't quite put the two mothers together. She is different from her family—more American than Russian. As for her being *Jewish*—no one mentions the word.

    The three days spent in Gomel were a whirlwind of activity. I felt as if I were being led by an invisible hand through a strange landscape. Figures appeared and acted as if they knew me intimately, and as if I in turn knew them, when in truth we really did not recognize each other was. My Russian comprehension was adequate but my spoken Russian only passing, thus making it difficult to adequately converse with my grandparents, to ask the questions I wanted to know about their daughter, questions about her childhood, her education, their Jewish identity and especially questions about how she came to meet my father and leave Russia. I learned little about her childhood or how her family had passed the war years. They were very saddened by my father's death a year earlier but did not speak about how my parents met. I knew Mother's feelings about losing contact with her parents, but how had it been for them to have their daughter and granddaughter leave Russia and for eighteen years not know whether they were dead or alive? One thing was certain; from the time my mother was a young girl, my grandparents, aunts, uncles and cousins admired her for her intelligence, good looks, determination, and lively spirit. During my visit I heard much praise showered on her. At the same time, there must have been feelings of hurt as well as envy as she had escaped their fate by not remaining in Russia and making her life in America.

    The language barrier added to the strangeness of it all. I felt overwhelmed with feelings as each new relative I met looked stunned, grabbed, hugged, and kissed me. I was in shock, bewildered: The visit after all offered only a very small window into my mother's past.

    One feeling I could identify in the midst of this confusion was unbearable guilt. At times it was as if I could not breathe. I was pained, seeing how my family lived. When relatives questioned me about our home in Chicago, I found it impossible to admit that we had separate bedrooms, two bathrooms, a dining room, living room, and additional rooms with no particular function. Any description I could offer would have been unimaginable to them. I found myself playing down my home, or that it was a home we owned. In truth, it reminded me of a story I frequently heard as a child living in Germany before coming to America. "In America the streets are paved with gold." As a child I did not hear this as a metaphor but took it literally. Being in Gomel, I felt the streets in America might as well have been paved with gold.

They were astonished to hear that I would be meeting a friend in Paris and that together we would be travelling all through Europe, and that after our trip I would return home, enter graduate school, and move into my own apartment. They could not comprehend that I would be moving away from home, living on my own. *Boze moi*—Oh, my God—they exclaimed! The idea that I was free to travel whenever and wherever I wished was as unimaginable as was the idea that I would want to live apart from my family. They would shake their heads in disbelief at what they heard saying, *Ya ne mogu eto poverit*—I can't believe what you are saying.

As Gomel is the oldest Belarusian town situated on the southeastern part of Russia, on the bank of the Sozh river, I was also treated as a tourist. We strolled through the park, admiring monuments including the important architectural Gomel Palace and Park Ensemble, an old noble estate designated as a historical-cultural site. The city parks play a central role in the lives of Russians. They are very proud of these parks and use them as a respite from their crowded homes with their lack of privacy. We walked along tree-lined paths, elaborate plantings and arranged flowers beds displaying vibrant red, yellow and white blossoms. My relatives were happy to point out the many statues and monuments ubiquitous to all Russian cities and towns.

In the late 80s my cousin Alex was invited by my mother to visit the US, and when he arrived I picked him up at the airport. The next morning I took him for a jog in Riverside Park. He kept stopping at all the statues and memorials, asking me to tell him the names of the figures and their history. I was at first annoyed by this frequent stopping since it was not how one customarily went for a run. As we stood in front of one or another figure, I felt perplexed as well as embarrassed because not only had I never noticed many of these sculptures and memorials but I knew little about their history. I realized later that of course this Russian cousin would notice these commemoratives and want to know their history. This interest in monuments was quintessential Soviet, serving the purpose of glorifying the Revolution and Soviet life. One of the biggest attractions in Moscow's Red Square is Lenin's Tomb where his embalmed body has been resting since 1924.

The parks serve another important function of providing a place for private conversations among citizens without the fear of someone eves dropping. In Yalta, walking on a boardwalk along the Black Sea, I gained enough courage to ask one of my mother's older relatives about whether or not he felt Communism has been good for Russians. He pointed to the feet of the people passing and said, Prior to the revolution they wore sackcloth on their feet and now they have shoes. And while he admitted that life was very difficult in Russia, it was better than before the revolution.

Apart from visiting the parks, much of the time was spent with family friends who were invited to meet the unusual guest. More meals were served, including caviar accompanied by Russian *Champagne*. And as in Moscow, Leningrad and Yalta, everyone was eager for news of America. The questions centered on the assassination of President Kennedy, our political demonstrations, racial problems, the Viet Nam War and the gangsters in Chicago. The gatherings were always lively and warm. But as the visit was moving toward a close, I felt increasingly more fatigued, sad, and eager to return to Paris, to what was more familiar. What began as a very exciting adventure—my first trip abroad after graduating college, visiting the place of my birth, reuniting with my grandparents—was becoming increasingly upsetting as I gradually witnessed the reality of my family's life in the Soviet Union.

My mother's first cousin worked in the KGB and despite being very close childhood friends, he chose not to meet her when she visited in 1964, fearing that acknowledging an American relative might compromise his position. I was told that he very much wanted to see me but was afraid of the consequences. However, when it came time for me to return to Moscow for my flight to Paris, he'd had a change of heart. He came to regret not taking the opportunity to see my mother and felt pained at the idea of foregoing a meeting with her daughter as well. We met in a small park near the airport. It was a scene such as I had often watched in espionage films, although I never thought I would be in the cast. My aunt instructed me to take her arm and walk past a man who sat on a bench reading a newspaper but not to look at him as we passed by. I caught a glimpse of him as he lowered the newspaper. This constituted our meeting. I was shocked and saddened as much for him as for myself. I could only imagine the fear he felt, and it made me shudder.

I imagine our parting was hardest for Riva. We had been traveling companions for ten days, sharing adventures whose outcomes at times were uncertain. I had grown fond of her and felt grateful for the care she had given me. As I boarded the plane and turned to wave goodbye, I saw them all waving back, and I wondered when or if I would see Riva and my grandparents again.

I handed the clerk in Moscow my last remaining hotel voucher. The next day I would be on a flight to Paris, and I was more than ready to leave. In the evening I went down to a dining room that looked like an immense catering hall. The room was filled with hundreds of loud diners seated at long communal tables. I was escorted by the headwaiter to an empty seat at one of the tables. As I looked around the room and then at my table, I saw I was surrounded by a sea of male faces wearing poorly fitted gray business suits, men from East Germany doing business in Russia. They looked pleased to have a young woman join them. A couple of the younger men openly flirted with me and poured me a shot of vodka. I was enjoying the flirting when suddenly I saw the room spinning. The last thing I remembered was being held in a firm grip by one of the young men as I attempted to stand.

The next morning, I felt bewildered as a hand gently shook me to wake me up. It was the floor matron who was in charge of watching the comings and goings of the guests. Someone had undressed me and put me to bed.

When she saw the confused expression on my face, she explained that a young man brought me up to the floor and she had taken me to my room and put me to bed. Despite her coarse features and heavy frame wearing a uniform that could be a guard's dress, she was gentle as she helped me get dressed and pack the little that was left after delivering the contents of the suitcases to my family. I had also given away almost all my personal belongings except for a change of underwear, a new sundress, and my Parisian black bathing suit.

At the airport waiting to go through passport control, I thought back to the previous night's fainting episode, likely due to the emotional stress since arriving in Russia and the last image of leaving my relatives behind. Suddenly a new fear gripped me; the visa I was given in Yalta for my travel to Gomel was on a separate sheet resting in my passport. What to do about the visa? If the officers saw the visa they might start asking questions and I could again be in serious trouble. I was convinced that the only reason I'd finally gotten permission to go to Gomel was because of the kindness of heart shown by the police authorities in Yalta and in Minsk. I had no reason to believe that the permission came from Moscow. I made a quick decision and tore up my visa.

Once in the air, I had the distinct physical sensation of a heavy weight being lifted from my shoulders. It was the feeling of freedom… I had entered Russia and now was leaving. In my mind's eye I saw my family standing at the gate, waving goodbye, and I thought to myself how life is a game of chance. I could easily have been living in Russia right now. And then who would I have been? And what would I have been?

My first birthday in Russia

Sonja, second row left, and classmates.

With Riva at Peterhof Palace, Leningrad, 1966

Senya and me, Leningrad, 1966

With grandparents and Riva, Gomel, 1966

Grandparents, Gomel

CHAPTER 5

In Limbo: Ulm

What are your earliest memories? my analyst asks. The year is 1969 and I am now living in New York having completed my graduate studies in clinical social work at the University of Chicago and begun my career as a child psychotherapist.

What are those memories? I'm struggling to recall the years from 1944 when I was born to 1952 when I arrived in America. My mind rushes frantically in all directions finding it difficult to settle down and choose a place to land. Memories of those years are like snapshots suspended in time. I had often tried to will my mind to remember my earlier life, found it difficult, and assumed that my poor recall was due to personal failings. Slowly, painstakingly, and with the help of family stories and photos packed in a wicker trunk that carried our possessions across the Atlantic, with my analyst as witness, I began to unpack those memories and retrieve some long-forgotten footage of my history. Yet even before those memories were unpacked in my analysis, I felt their unconscious presence. Their presence accompanied me to graduate school in this same wicker trunk that once again served as container for my belongings. Among its original contents was a gold silk feather quilt with an embossed flower pattern that no longer wore the white linen eyelet cover. I still feel the heaviness and warmth of this down comforter surrounding me as a child. The trunk remained in my mother's basement until after her death. Today the quilt is tucked away in the linen closet of my New York apartment, but, from time to time, my eye catches a glimpse of the gold silk material and I'm once more reminded of the distance I've traveled.

Do you remember your dreams?

I didn't remember dreaming, but soon my dreams began to flow and flood the space we shared. It was as if he had pronounced the magical words, "Open Sesame!" I felt both excitement and fear, but it was too late to retreat. I was in the presence of someone interested and caring who was asking and *wanting to know*. Would I find hidden treasures or would it be Pandora's box? Over the course of my analysis my memories became alive and infused with feelings. Incomplete and imperfect as they were I could call them my own. Along the way I also became a convert to psychoanalysis. Like Dante with Virgil beside him, I entered the dark woods in despair and sought enlightenment.

In 1946 I was not yet two years old and my parents and I were living in a small village on the Volga River, close to the city of Uylanovsk. My father had finally gotten his wish to return to Poland, the home and country that he and his extended family left in 1939. The Soviet government had granted amnesty to former Polish citizens who spent the war years in Russian labor camps. My father made the decision to return and my parents and I, along with the rest of his family, left for Poland. They settled in Glatz and lived there for nine months. But resuming life in Poland did not turn out as hoped, because anti-Semitism and recurring pogroms made it dangerous for Jews. My father sought the aid of the Bricha, the Jewish organization that operated a smuggling network helping Jews flee into Czechoslovakia.

The Polish border guards were paid off by the Bricha and my parents and I and the rest of the family were smuggled across the Polish border into Czechoslovakia. This was the same border crossing that my mother described when she told of carrying me in her arms at night, stuffing a handkerchief in my mouth so that the solders *"would not hear you yell out in Russian that you lost your shoe and shoot."* This was also the time that we were separated from my father for two days when he had gotten onto a different truck. Eventually we arrived in Ulm am Donau in southern Germany, one of the largest displaced persons camps in the Stuttgart district. Displaced Persons, or DPs, referred to people who had been obliged to leave their homes and native countries as refugees, prisoners or slave laborers. Former Wehrmacht barracks along with private houses were transformed into homes for the DPs. Our camp in Ulm, one of several in the city, was named Sedan-Kas. In 1948, the number of registered DPs in Ulm was between 6,000 and 7,000. Poles, Ukrainians, and some Arabs also lived in the camps, along with Jewish refugees.

Like many others, the camp in Ulm became a center of Jewish cultural and political life. The United Nations Relief and Rehabilitation Administration (UNRRA) and the Allied occupation authorities were responsible for the administration of the camps. But ultimately a handful of Jewish organizations and the World Jewish Congress took up the cause of the DPs. The Joint Distribution Committee or the JDC provided food and clothing, health, and vocational training, religious schools, kindergartens and high schools. The Organization for Rehabilitation and Training (ORT) was a Jewish educational organization providing job training schools.

One of the earliest memories that I told my analyst was from the age of four, accompanying my cousin Elizabeth to the clinic where she attended a training school for nurses. This was later confirmed by Elizabeth, the story of how she was cleaning syringe needles and I watched her as she took each needle apart to sterilize. I was fascinated by the process and was asking her many questions, and then I picked up one of the needles and pretended to give her an injection, laughing and enjoying the pretend play. I remember how it ceased to be play when I pricked her and she cried out in pain. I can still recall my alarm and the tears that followed… I had hurt her, the cousin I most loved, and she was angry with me. Distraught, I ran out of the clinic and through the streets of the camp until I reached home. My mother was shocked at not seeing Elizabeth with me. Why was I alone and how had I found my way home? Soon Elizabeth came running into the house, distressed. I still can see her look of relief when she saw me, but her relief quickly turned to anger. She yelled at me, wanting to know why I had disappeared. She had looked everywhere for me and could not find me. Still upset, she once more asked why had I run away.

Thinking back on this memory, I'm reminded of my own acute sensitivity to anger, especially my mother's, and, in this case, Elizabeth's. My relatives and parents' friends were always complimenting me on being "such a very good little girl." For the most part my mother agreed that I was a good-natured, kind, and polite child. She gave one example when I offered sweets to my younger cousin because she wanted them and had begun to cry. But she also said I could be willful and disobedient. Perhaps the hypodermic scene at the clinic also showed an aggressive side to me.

Among many of the documents I have from Ulm is one that indicates that my father was seeking employment as a tailor and that he had to show proficiency by *"executing a test-piece in gentlemen- tailor's handicraft before an examination board charged by the Chamber of Handicraft."* The original document is dated October 8, 1947 and gives the result of the test:

"Mr. Berenholc is experienced in all works relative to the profession as a gentlemen-tailor and may be appreciated for this job. This certificate may be used for Emigration purposes."

First reading this document I was puzzled by the phrase *used for Emigration purposes*. In researching information on DP camps, I learned that the United States was not well disposed to admitting Jewish refugees, especially if they had not been employed for many years in their occupation, as was the case with my father. ORT established training schools in all the DP camps so that the refugees were in the best position to obtain visas to America. The certificate stating that my father was an experienced tailor and that it *may be used for Emigration purposes* was intended to increase his chances of getting a visa.

There is a charming photograph showing my father at his sewing machine, his face turned to the photographer, smiling. Elizabeth, her legs crossed, wearing a plaid jumper, is sitting playfully on top of the extended side of the machine.

My mother, on the other hand, did not go to trade school. Having attended a university in Russia and taught school during the war in Ulyanovsk, she was instead enrolled in classes to learn English. According to Elizabeth, she and my mother also took private English lessons from a woman refugee in the camp who spoke with a British accent. There are a number of photos of she and Elizabeth walking arm in arm in the streets of Ulm, carrying attaché cases—two attractive young women, stylishly dressed, going off to their lessons. One could easily mistake them for college girls, except for the damaged buildings that are visible in the background, reminding you that it is not an ordinary time or place. Ulm was heavily bombed during the closing months of the war and eighty-one percent of the city center was destroyed. I suspect that my mother would have been advised by ORT to become proficient in English, in order to have better employment opportunities in America. She excelled at languages, and when we arrived in the US was the only one, with the exception of Elizabeth, in my extended family who spoke English.

There is a photo of me in Ulm, standing outdoors among two long rows of children with three teachers. In the distance can be seen trees that hide the former Wehrmacht barracks. I assume the photo was taken when I first went to school since I look about four years old. The teachers wear light coats, the children wear coats or sweaters and, like a number of the other girls, a large white bow is pinned in my hair. Is it fall and the first day of school, or is it spring and are the teachers taking the children on an outing? I have looked at this photo repeatedly, yet I have never been able to call up a memory. I recognize the face as mine but have no feeling of recognition, no sense of connection to the child in the photo.

Only one memory stands out. Perhaps it did take place with the same group of children as in the school photo. I am standing in a large circle with other children. A teacher stops in front of each child, holding a bottle of cod liver oil in one hand, a spoon in the other. The children dutifully open their mouths as the oily liquid is poured into the spoon and into their open mouths. When my turn comes, I too obediently open my mouth. Now, simply describing the memory can evoke the disgusting smell and taste of the greasy substance. I imagine that then as now the expression on my face registered revulsion. To this day I can't tolerate the odor of anything that reminds me of cod liver oil. But apart from my reaction, and the fact that this method of distribution was not the most hygienic, it does indicate that the camp directors had the children's well-being in mind by giving them nutritional supplements.

Life in the DP camp was intended to rebuild and reestablish all aspects of Jewish life that were destroyed by the war. Living among so many Jews encouraged my mother to identify as one. And it was in the camps that I developed my own very strong and enduring Jewish identification. As a child my increased awareness of my Jewish identity was revealed by a story my mother often told: *One day you came to me and asked me in Russian, the language you spoke when you were little, maybe three, 'Am I Russian or Jewish?' I said you were Jewish. From that day on you began to speak Yiddish and so naturally I had to learn Yiddish.* To this day I can still hear her draw out the word *naturally*, spoken in English with a strong Russian accent.

My mother attributed my wanting to speak Yiddish to a desire to be like the other children who spoke Yiddish, the language most common in the camps. She always told this episode as if on that very day I had transferred my mother tongue from Russian to Yiddish. But I believe this transformation must have begun earlier. I had to have known Yiddish from birth because Yiddish was the primary language of my father's family and we all lived under one roof from the time I was born. In Poland it was undesirable to be Jewish, so the family must also have spoken Polish, which I most likely understood. In our second camp in Föhrenwald, Polish neighbors became our closest friends and they had a younger son with whom I played. In the DP camp it was safe to own my Jewish identity. My mother, however, presents her own account, claiming that she was forced to speak Yiddish since her child would no longer speak Russian. Yet she was the one who gave me permission to speak Yiddish. I suspect that what is closer to the truth is that my Soviet-born mother, surrounded by a large Jewish community for the first time in her life, submitted to her latent Jewishness. As she would often repeat when living in the United States: *I did not know about being Jewish. The war made a Jew of me.* Yet, once in America, my mother's identification as a secular Jew became fierce. For her it was never a matter of religion but more an identification with a community that had been torn apart and survived. She who had *no idea about being Jewish* became like the early Zionists who took great pride in the state of Israel. She loved her travels to Israel and would always talk about her time there. As for her several trips to Russia, she had little good to say about the Soviet Union and was always happy to be back on American soil.

In the aftermath of the war and during the time my parents and I spent six years in the DP camps in Germany, the most difficult challenge for them, as for other Jewish refugees, was to obtain a visa to emigrate. For my family it was particularly complicated because of my father's earlier health history. The authorities concluded that he had latent tuberculosis and thus was not a candidate for emigration.

A visa to Palestine could have been obtained, but my parents were holding out for America. They were not Zionists, and having survived years of war in Europe they were not prepared to go to another country that was in a state of crisis. In Palestine their lives would continue to be unsettled and arduous, and this turned out to be the case even after Israel was declared a State. I'm sure their decision must have also been influenced by my mother's thin connection at that time to her Jewish identity. My father, who was orphaned at a very young age, considered himself an atheist and politically a socialist. Recently Elizabeth told me that my father's longstanding girlfriend had been an ardent Communist who had been imprisoned in Poland. The choice of settling in Israel would have felt alien to both of them.

Historically, the overriding difficulty for refugees who were not personally sponsored was the simple fact that the American government did not want Jewish displaced refugees. Ultimately, it was the DPs themselves, coupled with the fact that so few countries wanted Jews, that put significant pressure on the United States and Britain to create a Jewish State in 1948. My mother's story *"Belonging Nowhere,"* in which she writes: *It all began with the end of the war. We belonged nowhere, nobody wanted us,* was not only her subjective feeling but also a political reality.

In 1948 the US Congress passed a law that exempted the DPs from regular quota restrictions, resulting in mass emigration from the camps. Elizabeth, my aunt Sarah and uncle Moshe and his children all left Ulm in 1949 to settle in Detroit, Michigan. Two DP camps remained for those DPs who could not obtain visas because of poor health or restricted visas for Jews. Our family, Aunt Tema, Uncle Lebel, and their daughter Susan were transferred to the Föhrenwald DP camp near Munich. In 1950 they left with their newborn Lilly for the United States and settled in Chicago.

For the next three years my parents were totally absorbed by the problem of obtaining a visa. My only recollection of that time was accompanying them to an administrative office in the camp and waiting on a bench while they disappeared behind a closed door. When they would reappear empty-handed their pain was palpable. Once in the United States and much older, I never gave conscious thought to our earlier plight, just accepting it as a fact of our lives as refugees. More preoccupying were my thoughts about my mother's separation from her family in Russia. For eighteen years she had had no word of them and did not know what happened to them.

Only more recently, in writing about our difficulty in entering the US, have I awakened to the abysmal role this country played in keeping out Jewish refugees. Looking back, it is hard to believe that I was not more aware of the political climate. Like other survivors of the war, my family did not focus nor look back on their difficulties. Our idealization of America endured; after all, America was our savior and my family among the lucky ones, and thus we remained grateful to the country that took us in.

I had often wondered about what my life would have been like had my family gone to Israel. Prior to the age of nine, I had no sense of a definitive country or place where I came from. And still to this day I hesitate in responding to a simple question such as, "Where are you from?" As much as America is my home and my country, the remnants of being an immigrant always endure. When I was younger I was captivated with the idea of becoming a pioneer and taking part in the building of a Jewish State. I planned a trip to Israel in the summer of 1972 with a friend. Unfortunately, my friend had to return home because her father became ill and so I spent the month in Israel on my own. I was astonished at being surrounded by so many Jewish people, it all felt so familiar and so visceral and it brought back memories of the years spent in the DP camps among all the Jewish refugees.

On a recommendation from an English friend, the American Colony Hotel outside Jerusalem's Old City walls became the base for my visit. As was the case then and now, the hotel is a favorite of diplomats, political figures and foreign correspondents. I spent fascinating days walking in the Old City of Jerusalem, returning in late afternoon to sit in the courtyard joining the other guests including the correspondent for the *New York Times*, who often shared the latest American news with me. We would sip cold drinks, talk of the sights we saw, and of the political news that day.

I took side trips to the Arab towns of Hebron and Nazareth and felt as if I were back in biblical times. I went to the Golan Heights, visited Safed, the city of Kabbala in the Upper Galilee and then south to Eilat on the tip of the Red Sea on the Gulf of Aqaba. I was totally taken with the landscape, the combination of sea and desert dotted with oases of green vegetation. As my bus traveled through the bright sun and sandy haze of the Sinai desert, I remember spotting encampments of the desert dwelling Bedouins. As I travelled further south, I saw the silhouette of St. Catherine's in the distance, one of the oldest working Christian monasteries. I have always regretted not paying a visit to the Monastery. It all seemed truly magical and I yearned to remain.

Moving to Israel was never a serious possibility, yet for a long time in my imagination Israel continued to hold the promise of a country where as a Jew I could belong. In 1973, during the Yom Kippur War, I seriously contemplated going to Israel as a volunteer. Equally surprising, looking back, was that when I told my mother of my wish to go, she did not discourage me. She too must have felt a sense of loyalty to defend the Jewish state. Ultimately, I didn't go because I felt too scared to enter a war zone. Since then, as the country and its politics have changed quite radically, my feelings have also undergone alterations. And yet, the refugee in me can still identify with the need for a Jewish state, although the person I am now also wishes for countries without borders, countries that encompass and tolerate differences. Being a refugee means that the place you came from has been lost to you, even when, as in my case, I can't name that place. Perhaps that is why I still wonder about who I would have been had my parents not left Russia, or had gone to Israel instead of America or even stayed in Europe. It is as if once a refugee, one's mind is always in search of refuge.

When the war ended my mother's American cousin, David Kravitz, an extraordinarily kind and generous man, decided to seek his missing relatives. I'm not sure exactly how this came about, but I imagine his mother, Tante Rose in Chicago, must have been in communication with her relatives in the Soviet Union and knew that my mother had left Russia in 1946. After locating us in Fhörenwald, David began to send us care packages of food and clothing. He performed the Herculean task of getting my father cleared of the diagnosis of tuberculosis by having his X-rays sent to Billings Hospital in Chicago, then on to the Immigration Department in Washington. In 1952 we finally succeeded in receiving visas for the United States.

Human beings, caught in the here and now of the present as they live from moment to moment, recover time past through memory. Memory and language defeat time." (Shaw, 2013 p.169)

I'm currently in a study group reading Dante's *Divine Comedy*. As an English major, I felt I had missed reading many great books in college and Dante was among them. Reading Dante, it occurs to me that this work can also be read as a memoir. Scholars do not consider it a coincidence that Dante wrote *The Divine Comedy* when he was exiled from his beloved Florence and had suffered a great loss. I feel that it is not a coincidence that I began this memoir as my mother was losing her memory to Alzheimer's, knowing that for her time was passing rapidly and would soon stop and I would lose her. Perhaps writing this memoir is my attempt to defeat time by recalling the past, to keep it alive in the present. For me and for others, the urge to write one's life story feels more pressing as we suffer the loss of parents and loved ones, of home and country, as we age and as mortality can no longer be denied. Writing our memories also carries the hope of leaving something of ourselves behind as we approach death, another way of defeating time. Re-examining my own life at different junctures in the journey makes me long for more knowledge. At times this knowledge and understanding may be painful, but it can also provide a kind of comfort, a sense of things falling into place, a new kind of symmetry and continuity.

So what do I remember of my young life in Ulm between 1946 and 1949? These memories are at best unstable. I'm often not sure whether the pictures in my mind are "true" memories, knowing that there cannot be a *true* memory since memories undergo transformation over time. Are the images or memories a product of the stories I have heard and the photos I regularly scrutinize? I love looking at the black and white photos my family brought from Europe, photos with their old world look that remind me I have come from a faraway place, that I lived among Jews in a large community where there were constant celebrations, weddings, birthdays, and farewell parties, all attended by familiar faces as well as by people whom I no longer recognize.

I especially loved the photos taken in Föhrenwald depicting my youthful parents in their handsome and stylish clothes (my father was a "gentleman's and lady's expert tailor"), photos of my mother having fun with her Russian, Polish and Hungarian friends, friends who were similar to the ones she had left behind in Russia. One photo is of her pushing a tricycle on which her best friend Edit is riding, and another one shows them licking a shared ice cream cone. In contrast, the photos of her in Ulm show her in a motionless stance, looking serious—I detect sadness and confusion on her face.

There is a photo of my father walking across a field in a trench coat carrying a briefcase, or wearing a handsome overcoat with a scarf tucked into the collar, his beloved dog Satan beside him. I can admire myself in early photos, including the one tinted photo taken in Russia. I'm about a year old, standing on a chair and holding onto the back. I'm smiling at the camera, looking chubby in my one-piece wool snowsuit and wearing a large red bow in my hair. Later photos taken in studios show a pretty child nicely dressed, with blond hair in braids tied at the bottom with bows and blue eyes that obediently look at the photographer. There are more photos of me sitting in front of an older cousin on a motorbike or in a woven basket attached to the front of my father's bicycle or standing on a stage decorated with flags at a celebration of Israel becoming a Jewish State. Even today I enjoy looking at these images that document my former life, a life that feels so long ago—so far away—so foreign. Looking at them once again brings back my few remaining memories of Ulm, memories I can now put into words.

A child of three named Fela, affectionately called Fegela, is not in her own crib today, but lies in her parents' bed situated next to it. Today the child is not playing with her doll named Schpringen im Bet [Yiddish for jumping in bed]. The child is lying very still, covered with a heavy quilt. She is feverish and appears not well. Her parents, aunt and other relatives encircle the bed. The little girl looks up at them and sees the worried looks on their faces. Her aunt is wringing her hands saying "Vey is mir" [woe is me] and her mother is nervously shaking her head and saying in Russian, "Boze moi, chto delat" [oh my God, what to do]. A strange man sits on the edge of the bed, touches the girl's forehead and uses a stethoscope to listen to her chest. He stands up, gets a small suitcase, lays it on the bed and opens it. The girl moves her head to look inside and sees funny-looking round glass cups. There are so many of them. He removes one of the cups and wipes the inside of it with a cloth that has a strong smell. He then lights a match, places it quickly inside the cup, and suddenly the little girl sees a flame. When the flame quiets and dies, he places the cup on her back—or is it her chest? He repeats this magic until her chest is covered with these small warm cups. All this time the little girl is watching his every move. After a while he removes the cups and she hears the sound of "pop, pop" as each one is taken off her chest. She looks down with curiosity and sees round circles of red and blue where the cups were.

A little girl of three wearing a light coat is walking with her father, who holds her hand firmly in his. A man is selling balloons on the street and her father stops to buy her a red balloon with a long string attached. He hands her the balloon, she grabs hold of it and within seconds the string slips through her chubby, dimpled hand. She is not distressed and instead looks with wonder as the balloon is carried over the treetops. She has never before seen a balloon fly so high.

There are crowds of people shouting, laughing, dancing, and waving small blue and white flags with the Star of David. It is May 1948 and the State of Israel has been declared. Two cousins, both named Fela, born a year apart on the same date, are lifted onto an outdoor stage, their undershorts peeking out below their dresses. One of them is holding her favorite doll Schpringen im Bet. They are standing in front of two small blue and white Israeli flags, shyly looking at the camera.

Aunt Sara takes Fegela to buy a chicken for Sabbath dinner. They go to the "shoyket," a kosher slaughterer. She picks out a live white chicken which the shoyket puts on a surface, then makes a blessing and with a sharp knife quickly cuts the chicken's neck, severing it from the head. Fela sees a bloody line where the cut has been made. He picks up the chicken, twirls it around his head, and throws it into the yard. Fela is amazed to see a chicken running around the yard without its head.

Fela loves to follow uncle Moshe to synagogue, to stand in back of the Schul watching all the men in their white shawls covering their shoulders, wearing their yarmulkes as they rock back and forth. She likes the musical sounds they make when they are davening, saying their prayers. Sometimes Uncle Moshe turns around and acknowledges her presence.

Years later, in America, she will make a yearly visit from Chicago to Detroit to see Uncle Moshe and Aunt Sara. Her aunt waits in the house, anxiously looking out the window until their car pulls up. She comes out to greet them, looking happy that they have arrived safely. They enter the house to find a big spread on the table awaiting them. Uncle Moshe is the overseer of a mikveh, (a shallow pool that is used for ritual bathing). Fela always askes to go see the mikveh. Her mother teases Moshe, "So Moshe, how is your swimming pool, can we take a swim?" Fela's observant uncle good-naturedly accepts her mother's teasing because he likes her and in Yiddish once more tells her that he does not believe she is Jewish.

I'm struck by how little emotion surrounds many of these memories. Earlier in my analysis I had been able to retrieve many of them. Recalling them now I see more clearly how they have become transformed and given additional meanings.

In the cupping experience I described my curiosity, but now in writing about it I realize I did not register the fear or discomfort I must have felt being ill, and instead I registered the fear on the faces of my mother and my aunt. Cataloging these memories and describing the little girl I was, I see her as if awakened from a dream, curious about her whereabouts but mostly a detached observer. My parents, while present, feel at a distance, as if they too had awakened from a dreamlike state. I now understand that they were still suffering the aftershocks of the war—their flight from Russia to Poland and to the DP camps. My mother who had left her family behind in Russia must have felt especially lost and bewildered. My parents were traumatized by the war and as much as they tried to protect me, their distress and sorrow were communicated to me and I must have felt all their confusion and fear. I had to protect myself not to feel the intensity of their fear so I allowed myself only to observe it on their faces. A portrait photo of the three of us is telling. I look angry and displeased, my mother looks stunned, as if caught in the headlights, while my father is smiling as if he is the only one cooperating with the photographer. This sullen and unhappy look on my face contrasts with the other photos showing me as an amiable child. It was in Ulm that my parents were legally married. I suspect this photo was taken shortly after we arrived there and for the purpose of officially documenting us a family. Almost all of the photos of my mother in Ulm show her unsmiling, as if she is thinking—how did this happen to me? How did I come to be here? Ulm was a stopover place for most of us. We were all still waiting to reclaim our lives. But my mother was feeling as if she had lost hers.

Kindergarten in Ulm DP Camp. I'm in first row, 8th from left

On stage with Cousin Fegele celebrating Declaration of the State of Israel, 1948

Family portrait, Ulm, 1947

My Identity Card, Ulm, February 1948

Mother & me, and cousins on motorcycles, 1947

Sonja and Elizabeth walking to English class, with bombed buildings in background, 1948

Sitting with Fegele in wagon wearing matching fur coats

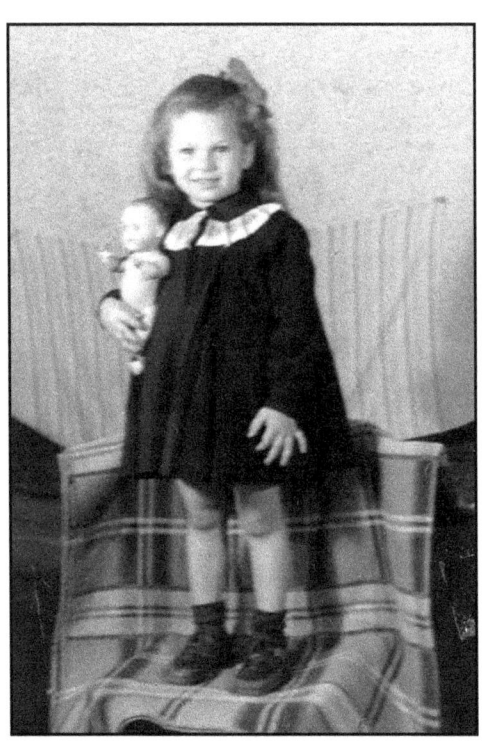

Holding my favorite doll, age three

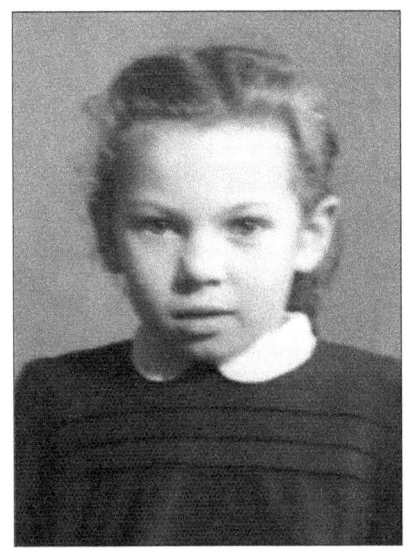

Identity photos of Sonja, Rachmil and Fela, 1948

CHAPTER 6

Föhrenwald DP Camp

In 1949 the camp in Ulm was closed and we were moved to the Föhrenwald DP camp. I was five years old at the time, and perhaps that is one reason I find myself confused about time and place. I had been confident that the following memory took place in Föhrenwald on the holiday Sukkot, an agricultural harvest festival. The Hebrew word Sukkot, meaning "booths" or "huts," commemorates forty years of the Jewish people wandering in the desert. One of the traditions in the celebration of Sukkot is to actually erect a sukkah, a temporary shelter.

We are sitting around a table inside the sukkah which my Uncle Moshe constructed against the outer wall of our living quarters. I look up and see the green branches and leaves that serve as a roof. My Aunt Sara passes holiday dishes of food through a window into the sukkah. My uncle chants a prayer as we wait to eat. It is as if I am in a dollhouse, my family joining me in play.

But the memory is not from Föhrenwald, it's from Ulm. How do I come to know this? Sara and Moshe were not in Föhrenwald. They left Ulm in 1948 directly for the United States. In 1946 I was two years old, living in Ulm, and Sukkot that year was celebrated on September 28. My family had no idea where we would finally settle, making the memory of Sukkot especially appropriate. As a young child I must have felt that the places we lived in were temporary. Even now, as I describe this memory, I'm reluctant to use the word "home" and instead use the phrase "our living quarters."

Other memories seem to have a similar fate; memories from an earlier age are reallocated to a later period in time when I had more words to anchor them. My inability to recall the actual physical move to Föhrenwald is likely due to the confusion of the many earlier moves. But more importantly, forgetting was my way of coping with the separation and loss of the family I had known since birth. And so I took my young life in Ulm and the memories of my beloved aunt, uncle and cousins along with me to Föhrenwald, abolishing the separation. The same distortion occurs in the memories of accompanying my Uncle Moshe to the synagogue to watch the men "daven," or pray, which had to have happened in Ulm. But in my memory the synagogue is moved to Föhrenwald.

Memories are fickle. Living in limbo, one location simply displaces or merges into another, robbing memories of time and place. Home was defined by my deep connection to my family, which wrapped me in a cloak of safety and protection. Even today my extended family lives in my mind, independent of frequency of contact. On my recent birthday I received a call from Elizabeth wishing me a happy birthday. She immediately began to reminisce about carrying me in her arms as a baby, and asking if I remembered the white fur coat I wore as a little girl when she held my hand walking through the streets of Ulm. In turn, I remind her of the Barton chocolates arriving in Föhrenwald from the candy shop in Detroit where she worked after coming to the States. Telling her about this memory, I once again feel my excitement at opening the glossy black box adorned with colorful bows and finding the prized chocolates inside. I hear her say "*Really, you remember?*" rolling her 'r' in her distinct, charming Eastern European accent. Larry, her American-born son, also calls me on my birthday to chat, and he tells me that Elizabeth has just become the proud great-grandmother of a sixth great-grandchild. He plans to take his mother to Cuba to meet her father's relatives, the father who left Poland and ultimately abandoned the family, the father Elizabeth never saw again. Stories traded like gold coins, relatives long gone but remembered and the past kept alive for the newborn to inherit. These are the stories and memories that constitute home.

On January 14, 2000, I noticed an announcement in YIVO's newsletter of a conference being held at the Holocaust Museum in Washington, D.C.: *Life Reborn; Jewish Displaced Persons 1945–1951.*

YIVO, The Institute for Jewish Research, is an organization founded in 1925 in Vilna, Poland, and relocated to New York City in 1940. Its mission is the preservation and study of the history of Jewish life in Eastern Europe and Russia. This conference was the first of its kind, providing an occasion to bring together survivors from the DP camps, their children and grandchildren, officers in the US Army who played a role in the liberation, Jewish organizations active in the camps, and historians of the period. Elie Wiesel was to be the keynote speaker.

On impulse I suggest to my mother, my cousin Susan, Elizabeth, and her daughter Francine that we all attend. Elizabeth and her immediate family are part of the Jewish community in the Detroit area that includes many survivors and children of survivors. Her two deceased husbands survived the concentration camps and the entire family is very involved with Jewish life. While my parents didn't belong to a synagogue they strongly identified themselves with "being Jewish."

I was always keenly aware of being a refugee, but perhaps entering the twenty-first century, two years shy of my 50th anniversary in America, made me more conscious of my roots and interested in the *Life Reborn Conference.* Since my stepfather's death, my mother had reinforced her interest in all things Jewish, including her two trips to Israel, the many books about the Holocaust she continued to read, sharing with me what she learned. To my surprise, when I called my mother and my cousins in Chicago and Detroit and told them about the conference, they immediately responded, *Yes, let's go!*

I hear the buzz of a swarm of voices as I enter the conference building with its dimly lit glass lobby, and I stop to look at the assembled crowd, men and women of all ages milling about the enormous space. I have no idea where to go or what direction to take. Standing alone, my body stiffening, I feel awkward and lost. What am I doing here? I stare at the people, waiting for the rest of my family to arrive. Some men are dressed in suits and ties, others wear jackets and open-necked shirts, the women wear suits or skirts and sweaters. At first sight they look like the usual attendees at my professional conferences. Later I will learn that many of the children born in the DP camps are in the helping professions: physicians, psychologists, social workers, and some, like myself, psychoanalysts. Some of the older participants are clearly old-world Europeans—I recognize their languages— English with Eastern European accents and Yiddish.

There are several tables scattered around the periphery of the lobby. On the walls hanging above tables are large printed signs displaying names of the DP Camps in Germany, Austria, and Italy: Bergen-Belsen, Feldafing, Föhrenwald, Landsberg. I don't see a sign for the Ulm DP camp, but when I search for a Föhrenwald sign, I spot it and walk over to the information table. I find a stack of spiral-bound books with the title: *Camp Fohrenwald: Growth of a DP Community—1945–1957*. I pick up one of the copies and flip through the pages looking at the photos, but I'm too agitated to really concentrate and I tuck it in my bag. Then I see tall pillars which on closer inspection turn out to be freestanding bulletin boards with printed and handwritten notes tacked to them. I peruse some of the notes—announcements of informal meetings, and contact information for participants. I'm taken aback by one of the notes, a message requesting information about a missing relative, and I find several such messages from participants seeking relatives or friends. I think in horror, all this time has gone by and they are still searching for those missing!

Standing there in disbelief, I notice that my family has arrived and are walking over to join me. They too look bewildered. We exchange hugs and kisses, ask about our travels to the conference. Suddenly a short, heavyset woman with dark dyed hair appears before Elizabeth. She looks intently at her face and speaking English with a distinct Yiddish accent says, *Do you remember me?* Elizabeth looks mystified by the woman standing before her, and she searches the face for recognizable features. Plaintively, the unknown woman once more asks, *Do you remember me?* Finally, a smile of recognition appears on my cousin's face. "Yes, you lived next to us in Ulm, can you believe!" They stand there gazing at each other like dazed, long-lost lovers.

I'm deeply moved witnessing these two *landsman* recognizing each other after fifty-four years. Is it possible that my mother or I will meet someone we know? Elizabeth now appears engaged and comfortable, while I continue to feel awkward and out of place. My mother looks restless, her head turning in different directions. Driven by an old desire to belong, I long to meet someone who knew us, the friends who played such an integral and enduring part in our lives in Föhrenwald and later in America. But I have a sinking feeling that I will not meet any of the people I knew. Those who remain are scattered throughout the US, Europe, and Israel. David, one of our dearest friends and also our physician in Föhrenwald, emigrated to South America, then moved to Israel and finally settled in Wisconsin. He has long since passed. Monic, our dentist in the camp and later in Chicago, is also no longer with us and his wife Vera died when I was still in high school. Even now I can call up an old photo of Monic as a handsome, young Polish dentist, with Vera in the dental chair while Monic holds a dental instrument, facing the camera with a broad smile. Edit, my mother's best friend, who looked like a Hungarian Sofia Loren, remained in Germany with her handsome husband Lazi. I still wear the gold link bracelet she gave me when I saw her in Munich in 1966. I hold on to just a little hope that perhaps one of them will be here. Maybe our neighbor Malgosha with whom we shared our living quarters in the camp? She now lives in New Jersey. I don't know where her son Samush lives. I was six when he was about two in Föhrenwald. But I will not meet her husband Iza, the principal at the school I attended in the camp. He passed away some time ago.

Do you remember me? I remember all of them as if time stood still.

My mother and I share a room. I sit in the armchair while she lies down on her bed to take a nap. Restless and wound up, I can't sleep but suddenly I remember the book I picked up at the desk. I find it in my bag, take it over to my own bed, and lie down.

I'm struck by the spelling of the camp's name on the cover, which I have seen spelled in so many different ways. Most often it is spelled Föhrenwald, but here it is Fohrenwald without an umlaut. Family names and places of birth were frequently changed, countries were given new names as borders changed or shifted, passed back and forth like trading cards. I myself was given different names depending on the country where we lived, called an assortment of names—Fegele in Yiddish, Felicia in German and Phyllis in English. On documents my father's name was spelled variously, *Rachmil Berenholc, Rachmal Berenholtz*, etc. Recently when I saw the manifest of the ocean liner *Italia* that brought us to the States, my name was listed as *Fela Berenholc*. I felt excited seeing my given name on the passenger list—it looked so official. But the pleasure was short-lived as my name was rapidly transformed owing to the caprice of the custom authorities and my parents' compliance. I stepped onto United States soil as *Phyllis Beren*, a name that has always felt strange to my ears. In the space on the manifest reserved for 'country of citizenship,' I recall the word *stateless* printed next to my name, once more justifying the hesitation and awkwardness that overcomes me when questioned: *Where are you from?*

I can hear my mother's breathing, slow and steady. Is she dreaming of the past? I let my head fall back on the pillow. I try to picture Föhrenwald.

What do I remember?

Jewish life as lived in the Ulm and Föhrenwald camps was comforting; its daily customs, holidays, and rituals were all an echo of the *shtetl* life that had been lost. For my Russian born mother however, *shtetl* life was alien. The three years we lived in Ulm with my father's extended family felt foreign to her Soviet upbringing. I can well imagine how she must have felt landing in a camp environment populated primarily by Jewish refugees, in a family not her own and in an unfamiliar culture. Only when I was older, living in the States, did my mother share her complaints about her difficulties with certain members of the family. Moshe's daughter Leah would wear her clothes without asking permission, and my mother resented my father's silence and refusal to stop his niece. It angered and saddened her to be far removed from her own family, not knowing their fate while witnessing her husband's close ties to his own family. She imagined he put them first, making her feel that much more the outsider. In hindsight, I wonder if she began to feel disappointed in my father in Ulm, a disappointment which increased during their lives together. Perhaps some of those feelings of jealousy and resentment about my father's loyalty to his family were driven by an underlying guilt. She had abandoned her own family by leaving Russia and the loss weighed on her. Her frequent cry that she was an orphan seemed to me to be the punishment for leaving them behind.

I now understand that my mother's connection to her own Jewishness took many years to evolve. Her conscious awareness of being a Jew must have surfaced after the Germans invaded Gomel and her family was forced to flee from their home. With the ending of the war, when we left Russia with my father's family to return to Poland, she must have felt her identity shift again, leaving her family in Russia. Our stay of nine months in Poland ended when the entire family was once more forced to escape the Polish *pogroms* and we were smuggled across the border into Czechoslovakia, eventually to the DP camp in Ulm. In all these moves, I imagine my mother's inner life as chaotic.

In Ulm, *shtetl* life was seeping in and my mother's life as a Jew more fully emerged. It was in Ulm that I asked my mother, *am I Russian or Jewish?* And in Ulm she answered, *you are Jewish.* Later in Föhrenwald she would call me the *Rebbetzin* (*the Rabbi's wife*), because I liked to go to synagogue. In Föhrenwald my father's Great Dane, Satan, howled seconds before the siren was heard announcing the Sabbath and my mother would jokingly say we had a Sabbath dog. Fifty years later she declared her Russian-Blue cat, Verushka, to be Jewish because the cat liked gefilte fish. The woman who frequently exclaimed, *I did not know I was Jewish until the war broke out,* came to draw comfort and pride from being a Jew.

Suddenly alert in my bed in the hotel room, I feel something pressing on my chest. Looking down I see the book about Föhrenwald. My mother is still lying on her back in bed fast asleep, a petite, shapely figure with an attractive face and flawless complexion that belies her years.

On the cover of *Camp Fohrenwald: Growth of a DP Community—1945–1957* is a grainy black and white photograph that shows an entrance sign on one side of a dirt road leading into the camp: *Regierungslager—Fur Heimat Auslander—Fohrenwald.* Scraggly looking trees are planted near the road as if trying to hide the camp from view. There is a suggestion of a metal fence in front of a field; in the distance there are buildings with pitched roofs. The quality of the photo is so poor that I can't tell whether the fence actually exists or I imagine it to be there. The first page outlines a very brief history:

The Fohrenwald Displaced Persons Camp was opened in June 1945. Originally a camp for DPs of fourteen different European nationalities, it was transformed into a camp for Jews only, by the United States Army with the help of the American Joint Distribution Committee (JDC). Fohrenwald served as a transition center for Jewish DPs, Jewish refugees from Eastern Europe, and Jewish escapees from the Soviet Union, until its closure in 1957.

Reading this makes me wonder what happened to the others who were not Jewish. Where were they sent? Or were all the people of "fourteen European nationalities" now identified as Jews making it a Jewish camp?

By January 1946 Föhrenwald's population had reached five-thousand six-hundred, and in 1949 four thousand Jews awaited visas to countries that would accept them as permanent residents. My parents and I were among those residents awaiting visas.

There were about thirty-four DP camps that were scattered throughout Austria, Germany, and Italy. Following Germany's defeat, the country was divided into four occupied zones run by the Allied nations: Britain, France, America, and the USSR. Föhrenwald was the last camp to close in 1957. By that time three-hundred thousand Jewish DPs had lived in or passed through all the camps.

Despite the limbo that existed as we waited for a visa, the three years spent in Föhrenwald paradoxically gave me a sense of stability and ease. As a child of five I was awakening to a new consciousness. The adults in my life were of greater importance to me than contact with other children, and I took pleasure in my parents' friends who showered me with attention. Living in close quarters with my parents, sharing a communal kitchen with our neighbors and friends dropping by to visit in the evenings, I was both an observer and participant in the life the adults led. My parents spoke about our extended family of aunts, uncles, cousins, many of whom had already left for America, and of their hopes to join them. I couldn't really understand our precarious situation, except on those occasions when I accompanied my parents to the office of immigration to check our visa status. Each time that memory returns I feel once more their acute disappointment, I experience once more my own anxiety that no visa was forthcoming.

Looking closely at the photos in the book, I discover they do not match the images of Föhrenwald in my mind. The photos show a war weary, unattractive place with ugly, soot-covered buildings and crude sidewalks lining unpaved dirt-covered streets. The gestalt is of a bleak, depressing postwar town, not at all what I recall from my childhood which is of a pleasant, safe, small country town.

Why is it that I don't recall the photos that are bleak but only remember myself looking pretty and well-dressed, and my parents and their friends as attractive and having fun? Once more I'm aware of how fickle memory can be and also how selective; I see what I want to see and seem to block out what I don't want to look at. I'm reminded of the photo of my mother and Elizabeth walking to their English class in Ulm. Despite looking at this photo many times, only recently did I notice the bombed-out buildings visible in the background. My focus was on the two smiling women holding their books. Photos evoke memories, and memories bring forth other images. Perhaps both vision and memory join in a selective attempt to erase unwanted experiences and feelings.

My mother is still fast asleep and I look back again at the photos in the book.

The buildings were originally built by the Nazi authorities in 1939 to house employees of IG Farben, and during the war some of them were used to house forced laborers. Once Föhrenwald became part of the American Zone, they were mostly converted for Jewish refugees, while some continued to be occupied by the forced laborers. The housing conditions in Föhrenwald were better than in other camps, with residents living in small but solid, centrally heated houses. The German inhabitants had been forced to evacuate. I can still also visualize the surrounding woods where we picnicked and the river where we swam and into which I once fell. I remember the house, its rooms, but most vividly I remember the people who were part of my daily life in the camp.

When I was a child the houses I drew always resembled the one I lived in. Our house was one of many rectangular stucco buildings with entrances and pitched tile roofs. My family shared an entrance hall with another family, each family occupying a separate room that served as their primary living space. Our room was located in the back, with two windows facing the field. (Here my mind is again playing tricks. I see the sukkah which was constructed in Ulm, protruding from a kitchen window into a field behind the house in Föhrenwald. Could there have been a field behind the house in Ulm?) A third small narrow room, adjacent to our family room, served as the communal kitchen where I remember a stove and a water faucet that only ran cold water. In the entrance hall were two toilets next to each other separated by a wall. There was no separate room for bathing or a sink to wash up. Instead I was bathed in a large tin tub placed on two wooden chairs in our family room. I can still see my mother with a kettle in her hand making trips back and forth to the kitchen, returning with hot water to add to the tepid water in the tub and recall the pleasant sensation of having my entire body washed with a cloth. I did not like having my hair washed. I hear my mother's voice as she rinsed my hair, cautioning me in Russian to tilt my head back so as not to get soap in my eyes.

A narrow staircase in the entrance hall led up to an attic room which my father used as a makeshift tailoring shop that held his Pfaff sewing machine. The room was the size of a large closet, packed with fabrics and notions which I assume he bought on the black market. Customers arrived by appointment. Often Satan, my father's dog, sat on the small landing in front of the door keeping watch. Satan had been David's most prized possession. I was surprised by my father's enthusiasm, because I had no idea that he was even interested in dogs. Later I became a bit jealous of Satan because of their closeness. My father said that Satan was a very smart dog who only growled at the customers who didn't pay their bills. He made a weekly ritual visit to the butcher bringing home scraps for Satan's meals which he cooked in a large pot on the stove. I watched with fascination as he stirred the stew with a large wooden stick. The pot appeared waist high when removed from the burner and placed on the stone floor, and I imagined the witch's caldron illustrated in my book of German fairy tales. I can still recall the most unpleasant odor of the boiling scraps and a feeling of disgust. Satan was a "man's dog," and I was both in awe and a bit scared of him. But my father and Satan loved each other.

I recall with fear an experience when I was playing on the top landing of the staircase where my mother was ironing. She did not join my pretend tea party. I was setting out my miniature white porcelain tea set decorated with pink flowers when one of the cups suddenly fell down the stairs. I bent over to retrieve it and tumbled head first down the stairs. In the split second before I fell, I knew that my mother would be angry with me if the cup broke. I can still feel the curve of my back as I turned over several times trying to stop my fall by grabbing the rails of the bannister, hearing my mother's screams close behind. Miraculously, I was fine, but my mother was totally distraught as she finally caught up with me and held me in her arms.

The United States Holocaust Museum website says that within fifteen months of the camp's opening two hundred women were pregnant. No wonder I sensed the sexually-charged air around me. My parents' friends were an attractive, lively group of young people who enjoyed having a good time—some single, others recently married, some with babies on the way. Reaching a place of safety rekindled their sexuality. After years of terror, a sense of aliveness replaced dread and hopelessness, people began to feel human once more. It was in this atmosphere, between the ages of five and nine, that I became more conscious of my own emerging sexual curiosity.

In the center of our room on California Street stood a dining table covered with a cloth, surrounded be a few chairs. My parents' bed stood against a wall. A curtain hung from a rod at the foot of the bed, separating their bed from my smaller one on the adjoining wall. Living in such close quarters, I must have witnessed my parents' love making or heard noises, although I have no memory of this. I can only assume that being a sound sleeper aided the work of repression.

There was a small shed not far from the house, perhaps at one time a chicken coop, where I sometimes played with other children. I vaguely remember taking turns playing patient and doctor with a boy my age and feeling both excited and guilty. Did we show each other our "private parts?" I imagine I was curious about sexual differences but I had no knowledge about how babies were conceived. Like many other parents of that generation and like many parents today, mine did not offer any useful information on the subject.

My Aunt Tema gave birth to her second daughter in Föhrenwald. To my delight, my parents took me to the hospital to see my baby cousin Lilly, lying among many babies in the nursery. After gazing admiringly at her, I went to see my aunt and told her that she had picked out the most beautiful baby of all. I was six at the time. I imagine that some of my excitement at seeing the baby revealed that I had some understanding of conception.

One day my mother asked me to go outside and bring Satan back to the house. He was running after a pack of dogs. I grabbed his collar and to my astonishment he bit my hand; a scar from the tooth bite is still visible today. Crying from the shock and the pain, I ran home. My mother said he was running after a female dog because it was "that time of year." I remember feeling uneasy about what she was saying.

American films were shown in the camp, and my parents took me along when they went to see them. My own love of films, like my mother's, developed then. I can still visualize two scenes from the movie *Samson and Delilah*. In one, Victor Mature as Samson, his powerful arms outstretched between two columns, is trying with brute force to forestall their impending collapse. The second scene is of Delilah cutting Samson's hair as he sleeps. I knew that when she cut his hair she was taking away his strength, and I was terrified by her cruelty. I did not know the Biblical story, caught up only in the romance between the two. As a six-year old child I was beginning to have the stirrings of conflict and competition in relation to the love I felt towards each of my parents.

But it was not only insight into the adult world that I was gaining, I was also developing a sense of my own mastery. Like many other residents of the camp my parents had bicycles. There is a photo of me in a wicker basket attached to the handlebars of my father's bicycle in Ulm. In Föhrenwald I received a gift of a shiny new blue bicycle that I assume my father bought on the black market. I still retain the image of his holding the handlebars, running alongside of me, the sensation of trying to balance, then suddenly a feeling of excitement as I gathered speed and became aware I was riding on my own. It's little wonder that riding a bicycle is one of my favorite physical activities to this day.

Living in New York in the late seventies, in the midst of some life changes, I went with a friend on a three-week bicycle trip to Ireland. After landing, we collected our bicycles from the baggage claim, strapped our panniers over the back wheels, and mounted our bikes. Riding out of Shannon Airport, I experienced the same feeling of excitement and exhilaration I had as a child of six when my father took his hands off the handlebars and released my bicycle. This sense of excitement and mastery has remained as a core memory throughout my life.

The move in 1949 from Ulm to Föhrenwald brought a significant change. No longer living with my extended family, many of whom had left for America or Israel, a new circle of people entered our lives. Our living quarters became a social gathering place for my parents' new Russian, Polish, and Hungarian friends. Unlike my extended family from a small *shtetle* in Poland, educated primarily in *heders* or Yiddish schools, these refugees were educated professionals and secular Jews. Among them were doctors, dentists, engineers, and teachers.

Iza, Malgosha and their three-year old son Samush, originally from Poland, lived in the adjoining room and shared a communal kitchen. Iza, who looked like a professor with his round, thick lensed glasses, was an engineer. He was short, trim, and always neatly dressed. As the principal of one of the schools in the camp, he distributed the books that arrived from the Joint Distribution Committee (JDC) in America, and I was in the enviable position of getting first choice. A favorite was a picture book, images alternating with text, making it possible for me to follow the narrative of the story despite my lack of English. He was also an accomplished photographer and developed his own film. I have him to thank for the many photos that document our life in Föhernwald.

His wife Malgosha was very pretty, with dark, thick curly hair that she wore long. She had a deep lilting voice, often laughing while relating amusing stories. In contrast to her perfectionist husband, she was warm and seemed carefree. Living in close quarters you could not help but notice their arguments. Iza would routinely be annoyed by Malgosha's housekeeping and her general laissez-faire attitude. My parents marveled at their different personalities. I liked them both very much and enjoyed spending time with them.

The two families got along exceedingly well, becoming close friends. Iza was probably the one who arranged many of the outings and tours that our group of friends took outside the confines of the camp. It was fairly common in the summer to venture out for an afternoon, to picnic and swim in a river hidden away in the surrounding forest. Etched in my memory is one of those afternoons.

One day, my parents and their friends were picnicking when I wandered away from them and walked a short distance to a swimming area on the river. A large T-shaped pipe extended from the bank of the river and people sat on that pipe, dangling their legs and splashing their feet in the water below. I climbed onto the pipe and sat down next to one of the gym teachers I recognized from school. My legs did not reach the top of the water. He asked, "Do you know how to swim, what happens if you fall in?" I answered something to the effect of, "I will have to learn." At that moment I lost my precarious balance, slipped into the water, felt myself going under and just as quickly, I felt two strong hands grabbing my outstretched arms and pulling me up. I remember looking at the teacher feeling more shame than fear, sensing I had been cocky, showing off, knowing I should not have climbed onto the pipe. Dripping water as I walked, fearful of my parents finding out, I returned to the blanket deciding not to tell them about the incident. I was afraid of my mother's anger, knowing she was especially worried about my safety. I also felt guilty at keeping a secret from them since I was generally a very "good and obedient child," as my mother often noted.

This makes me think of another terrifying scene involving Samush. Along with some other friends, our two families were gathered in our room around the table playing cards. Satan was lying on the floor nearby, and Samush kept pulling at his collar. I would imagine that the grown-ups must have told Samush to stop annoying the dog, but he did not stop and repeated the teasing. Suddenly Satan lunged at his face and bit him. I can still see the sight of blood and Samush being rushed to the hospital nearby. He was very lucky because the attack missed his eye, but not without leaving a visible scar.

David was my parents' closest friend and I was very attached to him. He was a tall Russian, with black hair and intense dark eyes, charismatic, very intelligent, and musically talented. He had two very distinct sides. He could be stern, imposing, authoritarian, but he was also very generous, playful, full of jokes. He held a degree in medicine, had escaped from the Russian army, but found his way to the DP camp where they put him to work as one of the camp doctors.

David was the ultimate prankster. One day he came to the house carrying a full-sized skeleton from the nearby hospital. One water closet in the vestibule of the house had a small window that looked out on the street and not infrequently in the evening, when the entrance door was left unlocked, strangers could enter the house and use the toilet. David proceeded to place the skeleton next to the toilet, its head facing the window. I can only imagine the intruder's fear when he discovered the skeleton beside him. Even I avoided using this water closet, preferring the one without a window.

Unlike other significant people in my mother's life, she and David were of the same age and understood one another and the lives they'd led in the Soviet Union before the war. They felt a mutual bond in their shared language and in having been raised as young educated Communists. They also shared the experience of having left their families behind in Russia.

When friends gathered in our home they would bring along instruments; David played an accordion and we all knew he also played the piano. My mother, who had a beautiful voice, would join in on the Russian songs. At other times, they sat around the table playing cards, talking, laughing, passing time. In Föhrenwald, my mother was lighthearted, playful, enjoying the entertainment the camp offered.

I recall lying in my bed when I had the measles, David was examining me, instructing my mother to darken the room so no light would come in. On another occasion, I can hear my mother's distressed voice when I came down with the mumps and David had left on that very day for South America. I'm sure that her distress had more to do with his leaving, though it was made worse by my illness.

All these memories are suddenly cut short when I see my mother lying in the bed next to mine in the nondescript hotel room in Washington D.C., attending a conference of former DP residents. But I wonder, what did David mean to her, what did they mean to each other? Now as in the past, the thought of a sexual attraction between them had crossed my mind, but all I observed was the fond teasing that can go on between close friends or siblings. Their relationship throughout their lifetimes had a quality of family—the family they had both left behind.

From my childhood throughout my young adulthood David's life intrigued me. It seemed exciting and romantic. When he left Föhrenwald for South America, he must have traveled by way of Africa, because we received two postcards in the camp from Senegal. One of the postcards intrigued me; showing a dark-skinned woman, broadly smiling with a small child beside her in front of a simple dwelling with a thatched roof. The woman is tall and thin. She is barefoot, and wears a long wrap-around flowered skirt. Above her waist, strings of beads cover her elongated breasts. I remember being embarrassed by her exposed breasts, even more so since David had chosen such a postcard; but I was fascinated. Where was this place and who were these people?

David emigrated from South America to Israel where he specialized in orthopedic medicine. A couple of years after we arrived in the US, he wrote to tell us he had married a young Israeli Sabra. They had a baby son, and David came to the US for a residency, eventually settling in Wisconsin not far from where we lived in Chicago. His daughter, was born in the US. We visited his new home often—a modern glass house facing Lake Michigan with a short path leading down to the beach. The house looked as if it were designed by Mies van der Rohe and was furnished with Knoll furniture. I always marveled at the location and at the house's stark modern architecture. There was a grand piano in one of the rooms. My parents would often remark that he was too hard on his children, making them practice for hours, thus depriving them of more social activities. I was surprised to hear this because in the camp he seemed light-hearted and fun-loving. My parents' observations revealed another side of him.

I knew nothing about his family of origin, and he never spoke about them. I assumed he left them behind, as my mother had her parents. All that I knew from my mother was that he had escaped from the Russian army.

How did he come to Föhrenwald? I last saw David in New York shortly before his death in 1984.

When my parents and their circle of friends were not working, learning trades or going to language classes they would go on excursions. My father took me to a "bierstube," where I sipped the foam that topped his beer, and shared the smoked salmon on dark bread he ordered as a special treat.

I recall a photo that at first glance appears to be a group of tourists on a boat, but then my parents come into focus and standing alongside them are Malgosha and Edit. They are all smartly dressed in light coats. Father is wearing a silk scarf tucked into his trench coat, smiling, looking relaxed. They're in Bavaria being ferried to the King Ludwig II Royal Palace, Konigschloss Herrenchiemsee, modeled on Versailles. Most likely Iza is the photographer.

Another photo shows them wearing white pantaloons with black tunics and fez-like hats sitting in an open miniature rail train, dressed like the miners when they descended into the salt mines of Berchtesgarden in the Bavarian Alps.

Edit's husband Latzi does not appear in the photograph. A mysterious figure rarely seen, on the few occasions that he came around to our home I remember him as a strikingly handsome man. Edit's mother was a wonderful cook, and my father loved the dishes she prepared, especially her Chicken Paprikash; the red hot paprika would bring tears to his eyes. Edit and Latzi remained in Germany and settled in Munich where they opened a restaurant on the popular *Marinplatz*. Living in Chicago, we'd receive letters and photos of her beautiful baby girl, born after we left Germany. In 1964 on her visit to Russia to see her family, my mother stopped by to visit Edit in Munich. I saw Edit only once more after the DP days, in 1966 when I went to Russia to see my grandparents. Returning to Paris after my visit in Gomel, I met my friend Carol and we began our four-month trip through Europe. In a used Peugeot that we bought for three hundred dollars, we left Paris for Munich to visit Edit. It was the end of May and I was soon to turn twenty-two. Edit greeted me with an embrace and the beautiful smile that I remembered from childhood.

While in Munich, Edit agreed to drive us to Föhernwald. Stopping at what had been our house on the street then called *California*, I felt confused and disoriented. The house was not as I recalled it from memory—an unadorned gray stucco building. Instead I saw a white-washed house with small windows sporting window boxes filled with colorful flowers, and in front a patch of green lawn. The street was as unfamiliar as the surroundings. It must have resumed the tidy German-town existence it had held before the war, leaving little trace of its former life as the Föhrenwald Displaced Persons Camp where I had spent four years. Driving back to Munich, I felt an eerie detachment, an eagerness to escape the place and move on to our next stop, traveling to countries that held no memories of the past. I wanted my European adventure to be like those of other young American college graduates.

Now, looking back, I see I must already have been in a state of emotional overload. My visit to Föhrenwald came on the heels of my overwhelming experience in Russia, the reunion with my grandparents and other relatives, seeing the conditions of their lives in the Soviet Union and the immense guilt I had felt witnessing the sharp contrast between their lives and my family's comfortable existence in the US. I was still partly in the emotional grip of that visit, the connection to my mother and her mourning for the loss of her parents, the return of the feelings of my own childhood. I had always wanted to know more about my mother, where she had come from, who her parents were, who she had been before she was my mother.

Recently I found a postcard I'd sent from Germany to my mother and Charles, my step-father.

Hi Mom and Chuck,

Carol & I just spent our time in this beautiful castle. If I remember, mother, you too have been to Chiemsee. Right now we are in Saltzberg, Austria—after we will go to Vienna. Both of us are having a wonderful time. Last night I had

dinner at Edit's & met Lacy, Yulek and the rest. It was wonderful seeing all of them, but everybody talked about you so much that I got homesick.
   Bye for now & much love, Pips

After Salzburg we had gone to Berchtesgaden where the photo of my parents and their friends wearing the miners' clothes had been taken. I documented the occasion with a photo of my own, sitting in a small car train ready to descend into the coal mines.

Hitler's mountain residence was located near Berchtesgarden, an outpost for the Third Reich. Kehlsteinhaus, nicknamed "Eagle's Nest," was built in 1939 as a present for Hitler's birthday. US soldiers captured Berchtesgaden in 1945, and it became a holiday and recreation retreat for the American military. I can still see the tourist guide pointing high up a mountain to the "Eagle's Nest," and I can still feel my body shudder as I looked up. It also reminded me of a building in Föhrenwald. I was afraid to pass because jutting out from the top was a column with the outline of a painted Swastika. While I spoke some German, I was very uncomfortable when asked questions, fearing the mixture of Yiddish and German in my speech would be detected. I had little desire to see more of Germany.

Germany as a country can even now provoke a reaction in me. Yet, at the same time. when someone asks what life was like in the DP camps, I have no difficulty replying that for the most part my memories are good ones—memories of belonging, of familiarity, of comfort, of a child having fun and discovering the world around her.

I did return to Germany when the Berlin Wall came down, heralding the collapse of the Soviet Union's hold over the Eastern European countries. I wanted once more to witness a border changing hands, perhaps because I also wanted the wall between the past and present to come down.

To my surprise, I learned that in the summer of 2016 a photo exhibition was shown in Frankfurt entitled *The Children of DP Camp Föhrenwald*. The photos on the website looked like the many photos I own depicting life in the camp; adults at work, in training schools, in classes learning languages, playing sports, celebrating weddings and births. There are photos of children in school, at play, on outings, visits to the medical clinic, celebrating birthdays and Jewish holidays. I was particularly struck by the accompanying video in German showing Föhrenwald as it is now in 2016. An older married couple returns to the camp, now a very picturesque town. Smiling, they walk around carrying an old map of the camp, noting the American street names: Wisconsin, Florida, Roosevelt, etc. They recognize a number of the restored buildings. Speaking in German, they stop to explain the function each building served in the camp. They look animated and excited as they point out a building that housed the *mikvah*, a Jewish ritual bathhouse, and describe its function. Hearing them recall their fond memories of the camp, I'm surprised that my forgotten German is returning. The sentiments and impressions they describe are similar to the answers I give when friends ask, "What was it like growing up in a DP camp?"

I'm abruptly switched back to the hotel room when my mother suddenly wakes up and asks, "Don't we have to dress and go to hear Eli Weisel?" Startled, I look towards the window and notice that the sun has set. For a moment I don't know where I am. The book is still lying on my chest.

As I look back at the conference, I can see my mother's discomfort and restlessness. I recall her face, its frozen look as Elizabeth and the woman from Ulm recognized one another. Later, she became more agitated, finally insisting that she wanted to return home with the excuse, "I have so much to do, I have to finish the tickets for some clients." I was annoyed but also felt this was not atypical; it was an excuse she often used when she tired of socializing, preferring to go home, explaining that she needed "to be comfortable." But on that day, I felt something more pressing was making her wish to escape and run home. I suspect it was the refugees milling about her, bringing back her time in Ulm along with the sensations and feelings she had of bewilderment, of being different, of not belonging. Perhaps, further contributing to her agitation was that others at the conference seemed eager to search out and locate people they had known in the camps. Unlike those participants who wanted to remember, share their reminiscences, even reverting to speaking Yiddish, my mother could not join in the conversations, but could only stare. The few times she appeared enlivened was when Eli Weisel gave the opening talk, and later when she met one of the speakers, a client whose travel to Russia she had arranged. Speaking with this man she was engaged and at ease; he was from her current life, knew her as a sought-after travel agent specializing in Eastern Europe, and knew little of her past as a displaced refugee.

I now wonder if the intensity of her discomfort at the conference might have been a foreshadowing of Alzheimer's, the disease that gradually took over her mind leaving her with few memories. Like others with early stages of dementia, she was uncomfortable and anxious when the structure of her daily life was disrupted. Usually when I called to check in on her, to ask how she was, she replied that she was doing her bookkeeping. She obsessively balanced her checkbook and repeatedly looked over her monthly bills. And while never a very flexible person, she had become more unbending, reluctant to leave her familiar environment. I noticed that my mother's memory was increasingly less sharp than it had been, but assumed it was part of a normal aging process. But I felt hurt when she, who never forgot my birthday, often calling me at the eight o'clock hour in the evening when I was born, forgot to call.

Unlike my mother, I was excited and intrigued to attend the *Life Reborn Conference*, to learn more about my life in the DP camp. While I could not share the other participants' many recollections, I was deeply moved by their stories and learning about the world I came from. I have always felt as if I have led two lives, the early life of a refugee and the later life of an American. It felt grounding to be reconnected to my past, to have these two lives reconnected. I was especially grateful that I could be there so many years later with my cousins and my mother.

I recently reread *Middlemarch* and went on to read Rebecca Mead's book, *My Life in Middlemarch*, where she explores the influence the novel had on her own life. She uses *The Mill on the Floss* as an example of George Elliot's use of her memories to paint, as Mead notes, a "childhood landscape." I understand "landscape" in this context to mean the world observed by the child. Her remarks made me think of the "landscape" of my life in Föhrenwald, where I first awakened to a feeling as a being separate from my family, with my own sense of agency, discovery, and sexual curiosity. Elliot writes:

> *These familiar flowers, these well-remembered bird notes, this sky with its fitful brightness, these furrowed and grassy fields, each with a sort of personality given to it by the capricious hedgerows — such things as these are the mother tongue of our imagination, the language that is laden with all the subtle inextricable association the fleeting hours of our childhood left behind them.* (cited in Mead, p. 251)

And I remember the white curtained open window on California Street. I see the lilac tree and smell its wonderful fragrance. Beyond the lavender blossoms I look out at an open field, a forest of trees in the distance and I see my father walking through that field. I see the familiar pussy willow tree with its soft fluffy silvery catkins, that I like to touch and roll between my fingers, feeling their softness. Another delight—the day we discovered a litter of abandoned kittens in the cellar. I loved to hold them in my arms and watch Edit feed them milk from a dropper. Mead writes:

> [George Elliot] *shows me that the remembrance of a childhood landscape is not mere nostalgia for what is lost and beyond my reach. It does not consist of longing to be back there, in the present; or of longing to be a child once more; or of wishing the world would not change. Rather it is an opportunity to be in touch again with the intensity and imagination of beginnings. It is a discovery, later in life, of what remains with me.* (Mead, p. 253).

Memories are recalled over the seasons of my life. My early memories are reawakened in my present life, and these early memories are layered over the present ones and transformed. My current recollections seem to be in conversation with my past memories, often making it unclear who observed or said what. It reminds me of the film *Rashomon* in which various characters provide subjective, objective, alternative, and contradictory versions of the same incident. These early memories draw on my senses, the later ones on my thoughts and feelings as they become connected to spoken language. These sensory experiences, feelings, images, and thoughts are the infrastructure that comprise my mind, the interwoven threads that influence my personality and my outlook on life: loss, disappearance, and despair, and the opposite: reappearance, hope, and "Life Reborn."

Grade school in Föhrenwald, I'm 6th from left

Fela, 1950

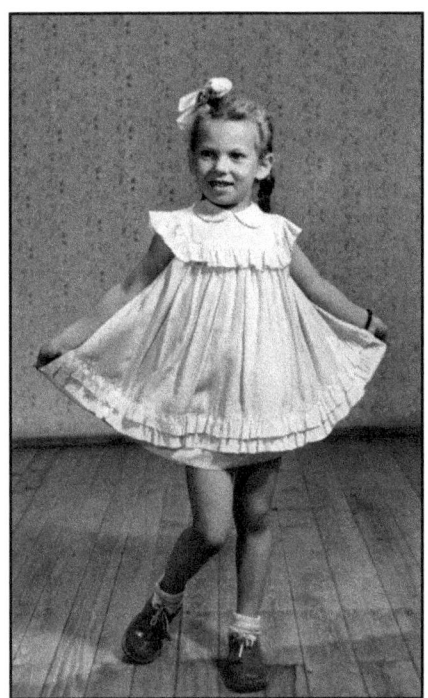

Fela, 1950

Malgosha, Edit, Sonja, and Rachmil, on an excursion

Aunt Tema with Lilly, Föhrenwald

Sonja and Edit share an ice cream cone

Sonja and Edit having fun

Mother with Satan in front of California Strasse 21

Sonja & Rachmil with Malgosha, David and friends

Father with Satan in the woods behind our house

Rachmil arriving in America, 1952

CHAPTER 7

California Strasse 21

October 18, 2018:
I am on a plane bound for Munich with my oldest friend Annie to attend the opening ceremony of the museum Badehaus: Place of Remembrance. The museum is situated in the former bathhouse of the Föhrenwald DP Camp.

This journey to my DP camp occurred by chance. I learned about the museum from an acquaintance in New York who as a child had lived in a DP camp. He introduced me to a woman whose parents had also lived in Föhrenwald and who was making a documentary film about Badehaus.

In September of 2012 a group of Germans decided to save this building, formerly used as a Jewish mikvah or ritual bath, and now owned by the Catholic Church and scheduled to be demolished. During six years of intensive work by a crew of local German volunteers, the old bathhouse had been reborn into a living museum-a forum for education and a place of remembrance. These volunteers were all second and third generation postwar Germans who were committed to document the history of World War II so as not to forget. They called this place of remembrance, Badehaus, meaning bathhouse. This preservation is the holding of memory itself.

I had written a brief essay for an online magazine called *ROOM: A sketchbook for Analytic Action*, published by a group of psychoanalysts concerned about the political climate in the US under Trump's presidency. Like others, I was distressed about the traumas perpetrated by the policy of separating children from their families at the border. The situation raised old feelings and memories about being an immigrant. It also made me think of my husband, a soldier, who had been drafted at the age of eighteen to fight Hitler. I felt strongly that we were in grave danger from threats to our democracy, of losing our moral compass as a nation.

A colleague showed my essay about the harm of such a policy to a US Representative and she in turn entered the essay into the Congressional Record:

"I don't believe it is an exaggeration to say that our country is now engaged in a war- a war to overthrow our democracy, a war on our constitution and legal system, a war on our principles, and a war on being human. Usually the first to suffer are the most vulnerable and defenseless, as we are now witnessing in the treatment of young children and their families at our border [...] As a child I had the good fortune to survive World War II with my parents by my side. We were together in a displaced persons camp in Germany in the American sector from 1946 to 1952 before emigrating to the United States. The United States Army, our heroes who oversaw the camp, provided a safe community for the refugees. There is no comparison between my childhood in the DP camp and the children separated from their families at our border. Today, I no longer recognize the country we live in."

After I wrote the essay, I wondered if other DPs or children of DPs would be interested in lending their voices to the congoing situation. After all, we had all been displaced persons once. I recalled all the borders my family and I crossed to arrive at the camp, and in my mind's eye I saw the manifest of the ship that brought us to the United States, where in the space next to our names for country of origin was written "stateless." It was after writing this essay that I reached out to my acquaintance to discuss the current border situation and found out about the opening of Badehaus.

I received a formal invitation to attend the opening ceremonies of the museum in Germany, and I asked Annie to accompany me. Annie has always been interested in the history of her own family's migration from Europe, and although she was not eager to go to Germany, she agreed to come along and support me.

Getting off the plane in Munich I felt excited to explore the city. We had rented an apartment for four days within walking distance of Marienplatz, Munich's lively main square, with its Neues Rathaus (New City Hall) and Altes Rathaus (Old Town Hall). With other tourists, we stopped to watch the Glockenspiel on the front of the Neues Rathaus, charmed as its mechanical figures came to life and danced. I was surprised to find the city so charming with its curving streets, beautiful palaces, gardens, and open markets. We had lunch sitting at a counter in one of the open-air markets, eating delicious sea food and drinking a glass of wine. I was a tourist, unwinding.

However, I also walked around the old city with a feeling unfamiliar to me, as if I were going through the motions of being a tourist although I had come with a totally different purpose in mind. Along with the pleasure I felt, I also observed a peculiar feeling of unresponsiveness. I was peripherally aware of not wanting to think about the next day when we would be visiting Föhrenwald.

Back in New York, when I first heard about Badehaus I felt excited at the idea of going back to visit my old DP camp. I had recently finished the chapter on Föhrenwald in this memoir, and I thought that a visit would be a fitting ending to the book. I was curious to see if being there physically would match my memories- perhaps even stimulate new ones. But now here, in Germany, I seemed unable to access those feelings. I told myself this was due to having too much on my plate with work and home life in the month leading up to the trip, that there had not been enough time to think about it. I was mostly aware of a kind of dissociation—an absence of feeling, but I also knew that my lack of feeling masked an underlying anxiety, a fear about not knowing what to expect.

As I strolled around Marienplatz, there was a moment when my mind flashed on my mother's best friend Edit who had opened a restaurant with her husband on Marienplatz after they left the camp. Edit and my mother corresponded for decades, but I no longer recalled if Edit, who would now be in her late nineties, was still alive. Before coming to Munich I had tried to find the letters she had sent my mother, but I did not remember Edit's last name and was looking for a return address on the envelopes. I had hoped to locate her daughter, but found only baby pictures. I thought that perhaps when I visited Badehaus, there would be a list of all the residents who had lived in Föhrenwald and I could search for her last name.

As I walked around the old square with its many busy restaurants, I thought of Edit driving me to Föhrenwald from Munich in 1966, how we had stood in front of the house, how it had looked different from when we left in 1952. I recalled becoming restless, wanting to leave and not to look back.

The next day, as the train left the Central Station in Munich, Annie and I looked out the window—tidy houses with back yards rush by. While Annie comments on the variety of plantings in the yards, I'm struck by how well-kept the houses are, their fenced-in yards offering a feeling of privacy. I picture the occupant relaxing in the garden, suddenly catching a glimpse of the train as it rapidly passes. Not at all what I've come to expect of homes next to train tracks in America, where neglected backyards are exposed. Soon we're in the Bavarian countryside. The train cuts its way through dense, alpine forests alternating with stretches of gently rolling green hills. Farms dotted with animals are scattered over the land. In the distance, greyish blue against the sky, are the Bavarian Alps. The train rides soundlessly on its tracks making stops along the way at small stations to discharge and receive passengers.

Seeing the Alps once again, my mind wanders to Berchtesgaden, the Alpine ski town I visited in 1966. I remember standing on a street in Berchtesgaden, and looking up to see Hitler's "Eagle Nest" built on the highest summit, and I remember feeling unsettled by the reality that one hundred and eighty kilometers from Munich, this mountain area was a large compound for Hitler's second seat of government and a famous Nazi retreat.

Annie turns to me and says, "P, are you getting excited?" I don't know what to answer. I'm aware that I feel somewhat deadened. "I'm not sure what I feel, A."

Within forty-five minutes the train stops at the Waldram-Wolfratshausen station, Waldram now being the name for Föhrenwald. We seem to be the only ones leaving the train. The station is empty. We climb down the stairs that lead to the street and notice that there are a number of local buses parked, waiting for passengers. I ask the bus driver if his bus goes to Waldram. My spoken German is all but gone, although I retain my comprehension and ability to read. He nods "Yes." Annie and I had managed to figure out the U-Bahn, Munich's rapid transit network to get us to the Central Station, so we had bought S-Bahn tickets. But we don't have tickets for the bus. Finally, I manage to understand the driver who tells me that I can use the S-Bahn ticket that I'm holding for the bus. I marvel at how efficient the system is—one can go from a subway, to a train, to a bus on the same ticket. A dark thought comes to mind: Germans are known for their efficiency. Waldram-Föhrenwald is only a few stops away.

The bus lets us off on a narrow patch of grass bordered by woods. Turning away from the thicket of trees, our eyes are drawn to a highway below. It feels as if we are in a movie; two migrants dropped in the middle of nowhere to return to the family village they left at a time they were too young to remember. We have no idea in which direction to go. Hoping to see a sign of life, we spot a highway overpass and decide to cross it. A small curved road seems to lead somewhere, so we take it, and after a short while we catch the sight of rooftops in the distance. The road indeed seems to be leading into a town. There are still no signposts to let us know where we are, but we do see a woman walking a small white dog. We ask her if she can point us in the direction of the Badehaus. To our surprise she knows where it is and points the way.

I understood before coming that all the old buildings in the camp had been torn down, only the bathhouse saved from demolition. I anticipated seeing a modern town with apartment buildings. Instead, most of the houses are part of units, no more than two stories high, with pitched roofs giving the appearance of small attached town houses. The houses are white and look freshly painted with bright red tile roofs. Some sport skylights indicating an attic. Each house has its unique landscaped small front yard with an iron or wooden gate leading to the front door. Some of the homeowners have even built small decks that hold chairs, tables and containers filled with plants. The overall appearance is of a small town or gated suburban community. The outlines of the houses have an eerily familiar look that is unsettling.

It's difficult to follow the directions as the street curves, causing the front of some buildings to face away from us. We stop, unsure whether to continue down the street. Suddenly we hear running, and turning around we see the woman with the white dog gesturing to take a right. I wave and shout *danke*, realizing I'm beginning to use German words.

Finally, a sign appears: Waldram-Föhrenwald Badehaus in front of a building that looks bigger than the others we've seen. A group of people, gathered on a large stone patio in front of a long table, are being offered cold bottles of water and beer. I assume these are the guests waiting for the last hourly Badehaus tour of the day. I spot the woman I was introduced to in New York and who had the organizers of the event send the invitation. She quickly takes my arm.

We enter a small room where two cameramen are focused on a petite, attractive, well-dressed elderly woman who happens to live in New York, a few blocks from my home. Suddenly the cameras begin to turn, and I realize that I'm part of the film in the role of listener. I'm disoriented, struggling to get my bearings. One cameraman fixes on my face and I don't know what to do, worried about how I look, not having had time to take off my coat or comb my hair. The woman begins to talk rapidly, standing close and looking into my face. She is very articulate, speaking English with a charming old-world accent. No longer aware of the cameras, I find myself drawn into her harrowing story about being a Holocaust survivor. I calculate that she must be in her late eighties, though she looks younger, and I interrupt her to ask a few questions. During the war she lived in an orphanage in Italy. She does not say what happened to her family. Towards the end of the war, the children in the orphanage escaped the Nazis by crossing the Alps, eventually making their way to Germany and the Föhrenwald DP camp. She had just turned sixteen when she arrived in the camp. Her words come flooding out, seared into her memory as she speaks of her escape, and I become aware there must be so much more to tell of her traumatic history. But I am growing uneasy about time passing, afraid I will miss the three o'clock tour about to begin. I find an appropriate moment to interrupt and say that the tour is about to begin. We all move on to the next room, with the cameramen following behind.

As the weekend proceeds I will hear many stories from the generation of children who were born in Föhrenwald, who brought along their own children and grandchildren to the opening of the museum, most of them from the US, Israel, and Germany, all bringing family stories of survival. About a hundred people attended from abroad. Few of my parents' generation are present as many, like my mother, are no longer living or too ill to travel.

I walk into a room that appears empty. I look down, and my eyes are drawn to a large rectangular glass screen covering part of the floor, giving the impression of a pool of water. I'm standing in the part of the building where the former mikveh was. A video is playing beneath the surface with Hebrew and German translations describing the history and purpose of the ritual immersion bath in Judaism. Traditionally, the mikveh is used by men and woman to regain purity after various events—for women after menstruation and childbirth, for men after sexual activity—as part of traditional conversion to Judaism, or before a burial.

As I stand and watch the video, suddenly the date of October 18 strikes me. We had left the camp on October 18, 1952 for America. It is October 18, and I've returned. Sixty-six years have passed.

Dr. Sybille Krafft, the President of the museum, greets us in the main exhibition room. From the moment she begins to speak, her enthusiasm and deep commitment to this project is apparent. Speaking in English, at times reverting to German, she describes the immense undertaking it took to rescue the building that housed the bathhouse and mikveh. They had to convince the Catholic Church to part with the building and the land, then reach an agreement with the local community to house a Jewish museum in the midst of their town. Prior to becoming a DP camp, it had been a town built for laborers who worked in the surrounding Nazi armament factories of

Wolfratshausen, and some residents did not want to be reminded of this fact. The project also needed support from members of the Jewish community in Germany, Israel, and the US. Dr. Krafft stresses that the project was to be a living forum for visitors to gather, a place of education and remembrance. In my decision to attend the opening of the Badehaus, I had given little thought to how this museum came to be. It was astounding to hear Sybille Krafft describe the enormous grass roots effort that took six years and more than fourteen-thousand working hours on the part of German volunteers to complete. The volunteers tore down and rebuilt entire building. The struggle for finances continues. The hours spent on documentation are impressive, including research that entailed travelling to Israel and consulting with the staff at Yad-Vashem—The World Holocaust Remembrance Center. This project was undertaken by a generation of Germans who want to confront their own past. Given my own desire to confront my own past, and my strong resistance to it, I admired them.

The exhibition contains photographs depicting every aspect of camp life; children in school and at play, adults taking classes, learning trades, celebrating holidays, weddings and births, photos of the medical staff and administrators of the camp.

Several video screens hang on the walls, each screen a grid displaying the name and face of a resident accompanied by a video recounting his or her history, arrival at Föhrenwald, and impressions of life in the camp. One man speaks about his boyhood in the camp, recalling the bathhouse with amusement. Since men and women used the bathhouse on different days, he and his friends would look for a small crack in a wall to peek at the women bathing.

I picture this group of young boys like any other mischievous, curious youngsters, the story bringing back my own fond memories of playing, exploring, and feeling happy as a child in the camp. There were many other such stories told by former DPs, describing a sense of having arrived at a place of safety where they could resume what approximated a normal life and begin to see a future.

There were also articles on display, donated by the former camp inhabitants; old suitcases carried throughout the war, clothing, children's toys and boxes that held letters, documents and photos. One man who came with his wife and children from Israel, whose father had been the camp medical director, brought two well preserved copies of the Yiddish newspaper started and printed by the DPs. He also brought his father's worn out blood pressure cuff that had encircled many arms. Remembering clearing out my mother's belongings, including the wicker trunk that brought our possessions across the ocean, tears come to my eyes.

Yet, most of the time I feel myself to be on a group tour, a curious but detached observer, uninvolved. I think I should be feeling more, but I don't. The other guests around me seem attentive, but their expressions are stone-faced. Perhaps they too feel like observers.

A pleasant-looking woman standing next to me with little expression on her face is looking at the wall of photos, and suddenly becomes visibly moved. She turns to me pointing to an enlarged photo of a group of men gathered to commemorate some important occasion. She has spotted her father among them, and is seeing this photo for the first time. Later, she tells me that she was born in the camp and left for America when she was a baby. She had not wanted to come but was encouraged by her friend, another DP. Like many children whose parents survived the Holocaust, she did not want to be reminded of what her family endured. She had brought photos intending to give them to the museum but felt ambivalent about parting with them.

Föhrenwald had been built in 1939–40 and served as a Nazi Forced Labor Camp for conscripted German workers and foreign laborers who worked in the ordinance factories in Wolfratshousen Forests. Many of these workers came from regions occupied by the German Wehrmacht, mainly from France and Eastern Europe. The survivors of the Dachau concentration camp Death March passed through this town.

In 1955 the Catholic Settlement and Housing Office bought the whole area to create homes for displaced Catholic families, mostly for those with many children. Föhrenwald was renamed Waldram and the streets given new names—the third renaming since the settlement's foundation. The buildings that looked eerily familiar when Annie and I first entered the town were the same buildings. They had not in fact been demolished as I presumed. To this day many of the inhabitants of Waldram stem from Transylvania, the Sudetenland, Poland, Hungary, and Romania.

I'd been aware for some time of a population of second-generation Germans who sought to confront their past. I have met second-generation Germans abroad and in New York, among them psychoanalysts whose families were once Nazis. One of them told me about a group of German and Israeli analysts who meet yearly to discuss the Holocaust. The writings of W.G. Sebald touched me deeply, especially his novel *Austerlitz*. Born in Bavaria in 1944, Sebald learned much later that his father was among the troops that invaded Poland in 1939. His books search for the roots of childhood memory. His father refused to speak about the war experience. Ten years after Sebald's untimely death, Mark O'Connell wrote in the New Yorker: "This reticence with post-war Germany as a whole is what impels Sebald's narratives of shame and historical occlusion […] It was Sebald's conviction that the recent history of his country could not be written about directly, could not be approached head-on, as it were, because the enormity of its horrors paralyzed our ability to think about them morally and rationally. These horrors had to be approached obliquely […] this is not so much a way of understanding the Holocaust, so much as it is a way of making us think about how we can't understand the Holocaust." (*New Yorker*, Dec. 14, 2011).

I believe that children should not be held responsible for the acts of their parents, so I've struggled with my own prejudice about Germany and Germans. Listening to the local Germans describe the effort made to conserve the history of the war made me evaluate my own feelings once more.

Badehaus was already performing its purpose. Annie was also struggling, her negative feelings about Germans still very strong. Some of her relatives died in the Holocaust. Her own parents were born in the United States, grew up in a small town in the Midwest, with little connection to their European roots. However, Annie was always curious about her family's history. Getting to know some of these second and third-generation Germans, hearing their stories, changed her perspective and some of her feelings as well.

Ironically, I was feeling more connected with some of the German hosts I was speaking with than with some of my fellow Föhrenwalders. In the U.S. I had come to feel agitated, angry. and deeply depressed about the rise of the far right, and attitudes of racism, anti-Semitism and disdain for immigrants. Now returning to my former DP camp, I was meeting Germans who were equally distressed about the increased support for the far right in their country and the rise of neo-Nazis. It gave me some comfort to meet people who felt that history should not be forgotten, that one must remain vigilant and involved.

The next day, we return for the official opening ceremony which is held in a church in Waldram-Föhrenwald. More than two-hundred people are in attendance, including Föhrenwalders, volunteers, townspeople, religious leaders, among them the Rabbi of the Munich synagogue, as well as prominent elected officials. Several videos of former DPs, now in their late eighties, describe in German their experience of life in the camp. A small choral group wearing traditional dress, sings Bavarian songs. A clarinetist plays a haunting Yiddish melody.

Again, I feel myself to be an observer in the audience, attending a professional conference. I do not feel engaged. The only time I have a strong reaction is when a young woman, a representative of the US consulate in Munich, speaks about the religious freedom we have in America. With all she might have said at a ceremony in remembrance of the Holocaust, she chose to present an idealized version of a religious freedom in America that is being strongly infringed by the President's in his racial and religious attacks on immigration.

The ceremony comes to an end. We gather in small groups to visit the town. Guides are ready to escort us to a number of buildings that served important functions in the camp. I see that the sun will soon be setting and

I want to find the building where we lived, but if I stay on the tour it will be too dark to locate. One of the guests in the group said they had found their former residence and that the number on the house had remained the same. Our street was California Street, the streets having been named after states and then changed after the camp closed.

I say to Annie, "Let's go find the house," and she runs back to Badehous to look at a map that shows the streets with their current and former names. I don't know the number of the house but suddenly remember bringing along photos on my iPhone, and I recall a photo of my mother standing in front of the house with our dog Satan. I quickly scroll through the many photos, my heart beating. There it is! My mother and Satan in front of the door to the house. I enlarge the photo on the screen and I can't believe my eyes — above the door is the number 21!

Annie is back holding a map with the name of the street now called Bettingerstrasse. We look up at the street sign in front of us, and to our surprise and relief we are actually standing on Bettingerstrasse. I walk in front of Annie looking for house numbers. The street is very long and the sky is darker. I'm beginning to lose hope when I see the number 19. Walking faster, as in a fairy tale, I see 21. In disbelief, I turn around to get Annie's attention.

"This is 21, Annie."

"This is it?" in an incredulous voice.

"Look at this, this is 21," I repeat. "Should I stand in front of it?"

"Absolutely," she responds emphatically.

"Should I go in?"

"Absolutely, you can ring the doorbell."

"It doesn't look like anyone's home."

"But you can try," coaxing.

I stand in front of a low, gray, weathered fence. A narrow stone sidewalk cuts through a small front lawn and ends at a red framed glass door, with two small darkened windows on either side. A few scraggly trees attempt to create a sense of privacy from the neighboring homes.

"Can you go in? Go in the gate," Annie orders.

I fiddle with the latch on the back of the gate. "I'm a little reluctant," I say.

"This is your house P. Was this fence here?"

"No, there was nothing here, there was no grass, there was nothing."

I step cautiously down the walk, as if I am an intruder about to be caught.

"Ok, I'm going to stand in front of the number. Do you need a flash? "

"This is all on video," Annie says, pointing her iPhone at me and the door.

I return to the street dejected.

"No one's home. Let's walk further down the street where I see some lights in the windows in the other houses," I say.

Two men emerge from one of the homes. They look related, perhaps a father and son, and they walk towards their car parked in front with some tools in their hands. They see us staring at their house, so I speak to them in English scattered with some German. I explain that we are visiting Badehaus, and that I once lived at number 21. They ask when that was, and I tell them from 1949 to 1952. The son looks impressed, as if he is about to whistle and says, "Cool." I smile, "Yes, very cool."

I'm hoping they will invite us in, so at the least I will see the interior of house identical to mine, but they are clearly in a hurry and move towards their car, pointing to the tools, indicating the car needs some kind of repair.

We turn around, and walk back to take a last look at my former home. I can't accept that no one's there and continue to glare at the dark glass door, willing it to open. As if in slow motion the door comes ajar. A woman with blond hair cautiously emerges looking as if she has just awoken from sleep. I move towards her and ask if she speaks English. She replies that she does, but is still looking at us uncomfortably, guarding the door. I explain we're here for the opening celebration of the museum and to my relief a lovely smile appears on her face. "Oh yes. I was just visiting yesterday," she says.

I tell her that I am one of the DPs who lived in her house. She looks interested, but makes no move to invite us in. On the contrary, she clearly doesn't want us to come in. I wonder if there is someone else in the house.

Finally, I decide to ask her if we can go inside. We stand there looking at each other awkwardly, staring at the door. Eventually, she blurts out, "I would invite you but the home is so messy."

This is all we need to hear; pleading and reassuringly we promise not to look at the mess, and tell her that it would mean a lot to us to see the inside. At last, she acquiesces and opens the door to show us in.

The house has undergone a makeover. The walls are white with light-wood doors and trim. To the right is a staircase also of light wood. The furnishings look Danish Modern. Many books and papers are piled all over all the surfaces. The living space is one large room, divided into a sitting room in the front and a combination dining and kitchen area in the back. We introduce ourselves and Elke tells us she is a Lutheran Pastor—she has only lived in the house for two years, having taken over the position and house from the former Pastor. She turns out to be a very lively, warm person whose earlier guardedness disappears, and for the rest of the visit she is extremely gracious.

As we walk from the entrance to the back of the house into the dining-kitchen area, I realize we are in the room my family and I occupied. The wall that separated our room from our neighbors has been taken down to make the one large room we first saw. I look around the room and picture where our beds, table and chairs stood. I gaze out of the window hoping to see the field I remembered, but I don't see the field, the lilac tree or the woods beyond. Instead, there are other houses visible. In my memory our room in the house was much larger. How did we manage in such a small room! Satan alone must have taken up any available space.

I turn to Elke, "When we lived here we shared a kitchen with our neighbors. Do you know where the kitchen was?"

"Oh yes." She takes me back into the entrance and shows me a very narrow room. The layout is as I remember it, the former kitchen to the right of our room.

I notice two closet doors to the right of the entrance to the house. Excitedly, I walk over to them, and ask Elke, "What is behind the door? I remember there were two toilets and one had a window."

I'm feeling slightly giddy and a little manic.

She follows me, turns the knob, and says, "These were for laborers." She opens one of the doors, now a closet. I have my hand on the doorknob of the other door.

"What is this now?" I look inside, and laughing, shout, "This is it!" The toilet I remembered, and a window looking out to the street!

Now talking in a very animated way and laughing, I turn to Elke, "This is where David—we had a friend—who was a doctor in the camp and because people came in from the street to use the toilet he brought home a skeleton—you know what a skeleton is? He put it in the window…"

Elke interrupts, "To scare them?"

I say, "Yes, exactly."

"A little bit like Halloween," Elke adds and breaks out in laughter.

We are both now laughing. "Annie, take a picture of the toilet." I stare at the toilet, again in disbelief and add emphatically, "Much nicer." And close the door.

My eyes light on the staircase I saw when I first came in.

"I remember the stairs, I fell down them," I move towards the steps to take me to the second floor.

Elke says, "Yes, they are a little bit dangerous, I always have one hand on the …," She walks ahead of me holding on to the railing.

"My father had a little shop, at the top of the stairs."

Elke looks confused and says, "A shop, shop?"

"Yes, tailoring…, "

Comprehending she says, "For dresses? Oh, look at this mess." She shakes her head as she climbs to the next floor.

"Annie," I call back, "Are you with us?"

"I'm coming, I don't want to fall down the stairs while I'm taking a video."

Elke says, "I'm so ashamed," turning on a light in the staircase, bothered by how untidy the house is.

"No, no, don't be ashamed," I beseech.

I stop in front of the room that was my father's shop where he sold fabrics and tailoring notions. I look in the room and see an exercise bicycle and exclaim, "It's become an exercise room." Standing in the small landing I see my father inside and Satan guarding the door, snarling at a customer who owes my father money and remembering my father's love for his dog and having to leave him behind.

Elke walks down a small hallway pointing to another room. "It's my husband's work room. We have a lot of books."

When we lived in the house, the rest of the second floor was a large empty attic with a pitched ceiling. I remember playing there alone with my dolls and tea set. Now the attic is divided into separate rooms. Elke is particularly pleased with the full bathroom.

I take another look at what had been an open attic. Once more I picture myself sitting on the floor playing with my dolls, and I remember that along with contentment I also felt lonely.

We return downstairs and go back to the kitchen. The tour of the house has ended, but we remain a while longer, standing around and chatting about our work, families, our respective travels—like people who have met on a group trip and find themselves compatible. It is easy to see that Elke must be a very sympathetic and generous pastor. I feel warmly towards her, grateful for the gift of letting me into her home. We say our goodbyes and she sees us out. It is now dark; she worries a bit about our finding our way back to Badehaus, and gives us very specific directions.

Later, back in Munich and in bed, I thought to myself, what had I been thinking not to come more prepared, nor to arrive earlier in the day, so that I would have time to walk through town and locate the house. To make things even more absurd, we had planned to arrive only in time for the ceremony. We almost missed the train, ran to catch it just in time before it left the station, and got on without a ticket. Once seated, we engaged in some black humor about the worst that could happen if the conductor discovered we had no tickets. I was avoiding my feelings about revisiting Föhrenwald, but my unconscious had clearly been active, resisting planning my time better, or coming with some Euros. It was the first time in all my travels that I had not changed dollars for foreign currency.

For the next and last day in Munich the organizers of the ceremony have planned a morning tour of the synagogue and an afternoon visit to the Jewish Museum. Annie decides not to accompany me, to take in more of the sights of the city.

The Ohel Jacob synagogue was built between 2004 and 2006, inaugurated on November 9, 2006 on the 68th anniversary of Kristallnacht. It is part of the new Jewish Center that includes the Jewish Museum Munich and a community center, an impressive building that stands in the center of the Sankt-Jakobs-Platz. The lower part is a cubic concrete structure of travertine stone, with a glass cube on top. The glass roof represents a tent (Ohel), symbolizing Moses' forty-year journey through the desert. The original main synagogue was destroyed in June 1938 and stood a few blocks away from the current one. Connecting the Jewish Center to the Synagogue is an underground memorial tunnel inscribed with the names of the four-thousand Jews in Munich who were killed in the Holocaust. Emerging from the tunnel and entering the sanctuary of the Synagogue—open to the bright and buoyant light of the sky—is shocking. Taking a seat, I'm finally overcome with emotion—all these inchoate feelings. All these contrasts.

I half listen to the Rabbi give a history about the building, the Jewish community in Munich and the current congregants of this Orthodox synagogue. It is not a strict Orthodox congregation and quite a number of its members have emigrated to Germany from Russia. Suddenly, I feel a weariness overcome me. I've reached the limit of what I can take in. I decide to leave during the question and answer period, not to return to tour the Jewish Museum. Instead, I call Annie to tell her I will join her for the remainder of the day.

The walk to meet Annie clears my head. The old city of Munich is a walkable place, and once more I'm struck by how attractive it is. We decide to go to Dallmayr, a famous gourmet shop with a bar and grill on the ground floor specializing in sea food. We find seats at the bar and order a selection of smoked salmon. Annie and I give each other a knowing look, Why not? and each one of us orders a glass of Riesling wine.

Drinking the crisp white wine as we wait for our meal to arrive, I push back thoughts of Föhrenwald. Annie and I are already thinking about and discussing our departure in the morning for Paris. She will meet her husband Warren, and I will stay two nights before my return to New York.

Back home, my family and friends repeatedly asked how I felt about visiting my former DP camp, just as Annie had asked on the train if I was excited to be going back. I still had no words to describe my feelings. It took two months for me to get some perspective on my visit, to understand my sense of detachment. Only when I walked through the door of California Strasse 21, did I feel myself come alive. I was reminded of my childhood, a child having fun, being comfortable and feeling safe, surrounded by the people I loved and who loved me.

During the three days of the opening ceremonies I felt as if in a dream or a movie. I experienced the other former DPs and their families as shadowy moving figures. I felt disconnected and ill at ease, not quite knowing where to situate myself. The brief conversations with the former DPs seemed stilted and dull in contrast to the more engaged exchanges with our German hosts, who were very enthusiastic and proud of what they had managed to create. But like myself the visitors seemed slightly detached. Perhaps they too were suppressing more charged emotions.

The mood of the group became more relaxed when visiting the second floor of the museum. One of the volunteers described the efforts made to collect artifacts that the DPs had saved from their time in camp. On the walls of this large bare room, the names of the families who had been in Föhrenwald were written in muted script. We were encouraged to send our family names to be added. Some of us asked each other about how our families came to Föhrenwald. We showed one another the photos we had brought along.

As we were looking at each other's photos I found myself seeing them in a new light. The others were amused by my photos but I was feeling uncomfortable. They were surprised at the photo of my mother and our dog Satan, not having imagined that anyone in the camp had a dog. Theirs were more typical family portraits or pictures of holiday celebrations. Mine captured an intimate portrayal of my young parents and their friends enjoying their newfound freedom, like the photo of Edit on a tricycle with my mother pushing from behind. The exhibition photos were more formal and intentional, showing life within the confines of the camp, while mine were more spontaneous, taken on excursions to the surrounding sites and attractions. Since childhood I have loved looking at these photos, and more recently they have been research material for my memoir. The photos contained happy memories of the camps, as if they could have been the beginning of a new life.

So why had I been disturbed showing them, hesitant to turn them over to the museum?

I had always felt that my parents and their friends were different from many of the people in the camp, but now I was more keenly aware of this. I was once asked how many people in the camp had been in a concentration camp, but had no answer. I listened to a video of a former DP describing his arrival at Föhrenwald from a concentration camp. A memory came back. My mother and I were walking on the street when she drew my attention to a woman with numbers tattooed on her arm. She whispered that the woman had been in a concentration camp. It was not uncommon to overhear relatives and friends whisper when talking about someone who was a survivor of a camp.

Many of the refugees like us who found our way to displaced persons camps, while not from concentration camps, had lost parents, children, siblings, and other relatives in the war or the camps. Many who were fleeing and hiding during the war were witness to violence and murder of their loved ones. My father and his relatives were shipped from Poland to forced labor camps in Russia, where they survived under grueling conditions that included freezing temperatures, heavy labor, and starvation diets. They were all survivors. But a concentration camp survivor held a special designation: Holocaust survivor. The whispering signified the unimaginable horror of surviving a concentration camp. Perhaps that is why when I was growing up my family never considered themselves Holocaust survivors.

Showing my photos to the other visitors I once more realized how different my photos were from theirs and how different I felt from them. Most of the other visitors had families with deep roots in Judaism; fathers or grandfathers who were rabbis, Zionist pioneers, staunch supporters of Israel and active members in their Jewish communities.

My parents and their friends stood apart because they were non-religious, secular Jews. My father was an atheistic Communist and my mother was raised under Stalin with little awareness of her Jewish roots. Their Russian, Polish, and Hungarian friends, many professionals, were also non-observant. Some of their friends were married to non-Jewish women. My parents and their friends in the DP camp had no interest in emigrating to Israel, whereas many of the other families did. This was some of what made me feel separate and apart.

But there were also internal conflicts, because part of my father's family, like Uncle Moishe, whom I loved, were also observant and came from a shtetl background that was totally foreign to my mother. So even before the DP camps, I had inherited conflictual identities that I was still struggling to resolve. Was I Russian or Polish, Jewish or not, observant or atheist; the daughter of an educated Soviet woman and of a tailor from the shtetl. These were conflicts that swirled unspoken in my family but were overshadowed by the shared desire to emigrate to America. Perhaps there was even some unconscious family fantasy that all these differences might somehow be merged, combined, and integrated in the haven of the American melting pot.

Visiting Föhrenwald, all of these underlying differences and conflicts were once more aroused. Once more I became aware of the feelings of belonging and alienation. And the earlier hope that emigration to America might lessen these conflicts became ironic, as I witnessed in horror what was happening in my own country in 2018.

In 2019, I'm brutally aware of the political climate in my country. My mood alternates between anger, helplessness, resignation, and a fierce determination to resist these regressive forces. My innocent idealization of America was supported by our good fortune in being allowed to enter the United States and make a life here. This idealization has once more been shaken. While others feel as I do, the feeling of being betrayed has its own intensity for an immigrant. I never took for granted the privileges of freedom. My family along with countless other immigrants who had withstood years of despair and uncertainty about their future were ultimately permitted to enter. Along with the scars of history they carried, many had the opportunity to have their lives reborn. But this country was now being severely tested as a place of refuge for immigrants as well as for its own citizens. This memoir was born from my need to remember, to recapture and to hold on to my own memories of the history of my immigrant family. But now many American citizens are forgetting that the United States is largely a country of immigrants. Turning a blind eye to this truth threatens our democracy.

I think back to my trip to Russia in 1966 when I was twenty-one, traveling alone to visit my grandparents who had not seen me since I was eighteen months old. I stayed in their home, visited extended family, and witnessed firsthand what it was like to be in a totalitarian state where everyone lived in fear. I remember later coming to understand that this fear also surrounded my mother when she was growing up under Stalin. Fear corrupts values, destroys idealism, erodes thinking minds, and robs people of their hopes and their dreams. As the plane lifted off the ground on leaving Russia, I experienced the physical sensation of freedom. It made me better appreciate the United States which, with all its flaws, was the best place that I could call home. My family kept the Holocaust in mind and would say; "Don't kid yourself, it could even happen here." The "it" was anti-Semitism. As a young person growing up in the sixties, I scoffed. After all, I marched for Civil Rights, Women's Rights, and against war—part of my love and faith in America. Yet today I'm fearful.

Because of the climate in the US in 2018, I felt more connected to our German hosts. They were going through something similar to what we were confronting. They too were trying to stave off the resurgence of their autocratic past and their country's movement to the right. What they had created made me regain a feeling of hope, gave me some comfort in sharing common cause. I was in the company of admirable, moral human beings, who were willing to confront their dark past, keep history alive by engaging the survivors as teachers. The achievement of a remembrance museum was a principled deed of activism and a triumph over denial. Respect for history and for memory are essential—culture takes time to build and takes but little time to destroy. Along with many other Americans who are able to face the past, who choose to remember and resist, I have not given up hope.

With Annie at Badehaus

California Strasse 21, 65 years later

EPILOGUE

Fela's Story

I began this memoir when my mother was losing her memory, knowing she eventually would not recognize me as her daughter. The realization of her condition awakened in me the need to answer questions I had avoided when I was younger, when my ambivalence stood in the way of asking. On those occasions when I finally brought myself to ask questions, they were was met with evasions or looks of confusion. The questions were about her, my father, their marriage, my extended family—our lives before arriving in America. Now older, with the balance between past and future having shifted, I longed to find those answers. Sadly, that window of time had passed—my mother's state of mind no longer made her available to help in my renewed quest. She lived out her life for another five years on the floor for Alzheimer's residents. During that time, I imagined her sitting for a portrait, sometimes patient, at other times restless, wanting me to get on with it as I attempted to draw a fuller portrait of her life and of mine. I began with those earlier unasked questions and searched for answers in my catalogue of stored images, conscious and pre-conscious memories and stories I had heard. I sought answers from relatives and friends who had known me since childhood, from photos, letters, books, the internet—all the while keenly looking at her as I drew. Ironically, because of her memory loss, it became easier to look for answers. I even felt some excitement, like a detective or photo journalist covering a story. It made me feel less conflicted, less guilty, knowing she was no longer fully present, since I suspected that she might not want me to know some of the answers I might find. I also sensed that in wanting to fill in the gaps of our shared history I would have to revisit our complicated relationship, including the feelings I'd always had of being her caretaker.

Could it be that the desire to write a memoir was an extension of that lifelong feeling of responsibility? It seemed almost natural that I would assume the task of holding on to my mother's memories as they were slipping away from her. Writing about our lives was my way of keeping her, a last attempt to recapture my lost memories, stitch together my own fragmented history and take control of my own story.

I never seriously thought of myself as a writer, although I did have a desire to write, having always walked around with many stories in my head. I have published a couple of professional papers, have presented papers at conferences, and edited a book on the subject of child therapy. I have thought of writing about a few of my very courageous patients, wanting to share their remarkable analytic journeys over the course of our many years of work together. But issues of confidentiality and the necessity to disguise material inhibited me, and even with the patient's permission I'm neither satisfied nor comfortable using professional language to describe them. It feels alien to the intimacy that develops from the deep work that patient and analyst do together. While I did not know this when I began to write, it became clear that in writing about myself and my personal history I became my own case study, with the advantage that the struggle with confidentiality was now my own.

My own psychoanalysis gave me insight, helped heal old wounds, and eventually prepared me to become a psychoanalyst. Now, thinking back, I see how it might also have anticipated and contributed to the writing of this memoir. It offered a method that I could use to reacquaint myself with my early history, a history that still remained inaccessible, hazy and confused. It compelled me to confront my ambivalence about wanting to know and not wanting to know, struggling with wanting to remember and alternately wanting to forget. Now, coming to the end of this story, I recall what I wrote at the beginning: My first utterance to my analyst was that I never remembered dreaming. My subsequent analytic journey paved the way to the *deep story*, the story that is necessary to claim one's own authentic voice. (Morrison, *Playing in the Dark*)

I have always loved oral history—listening to stories, telling stories—stories that were essential to my growing up. It occurs to me now that the most pleasurable moments of intimacy I shared with my mother were when she read stories or recited poetry to me. I see myself as a child listening intently, filled with curiosity and anticipation as the tale unfolds. Today I still get the same feelings when I read something I especially like and want immediately to share it with someone who might appreciate it; a way of re-experiencing the intimacy shared with my mother. As a psychoanalyst, I have the privilege of hearing many remarkable stories from my patients.

It seems fitting that this memoir became a collection of connected and entwined stories that built bridges between past and present. Some of the stories in my memoir are echoes of those stories told to my analyst and reworked over time. In my childhood as in my mature years my mother appeared larger than life. While her size diminished as she aged, and while the decline in her memory was the impetus for this memoir, it is significant that here she still holds center stage. The act of writing helped me gain greater insight not only into myself but into her as a separate person, not only as my mother. It is always challenging for parents and for children to view each other as separate individuals, outside of the child-parent relationship. But while psychoanalysis and memoir writing have a lot in common, they are also quite different. In psychoanalysis, the process of arriving at the deep story means experiencing raw, visceral, irrational feelings sometimes akin to madness, and only with insight does the fever break and greater clarity emerge. Writing my own story did not produce such madness, yet it aroused strong emotions. As the writer of my story, I was alternately the subject, detached observer, researcher, analyst, and patient. Being the observer allowed me the necessary distance to gain yet another perspective on my life. What resonates for me is the desire to get at the untold story, even when there may be few remains left behind. My mother's loss of memory made me fear that the few residues I held in my own mind might disappear forever.

In writing this memoir I came to have a greater respect for history, how essential it is to know and not to forget. I can't really know my mother's or my father's interior life, but in trying to understand them, their backgrounds, the milieu in which they were raised, and what they lost, I have been able to get a clearer idea about them and the history they lived through that played such a crucial part in my life as well. I now understand more deeply something I wrote earlier on hearing Elizabeth tell her story:

War with its chaos, confusion, danger, dislocations, losses, deprivations and uncertainty about the future leaves in its wake people who have suffered trauma. In seeking information and answers to the questions I had about my family's past, I was trying to piece together my parents' lives so as to lift the veil of my compromised memory and my own confusion. I came to understand something that should have been self-evident: My parents were traumatized people and I too hold the legacy of my parents' traumatic past.

Annie's daughter Jenny, herself a historian, who has always been interested in my history and who has helped me with the research for this memoir, has now passed on this interest to her daughter, Dinah and her son Alexi. Dinah invited me to speak to her 4th grade public school class about my experience as an immigrant. It was the summer of 2017 and the class was studying immigration, had visited Ellis Island, and relatives of the children had been invited to come and speak of their immigrant experience. My instructions were to say whatever I liked, and then the children would ask questions. I was pleased at being asked, but I also experienced an old unsettling feeling. Was it the discomfort of speaking to an audience about being a refugee?

An old memory returns.

When we first arrived in Chicago from Germany we moved into an apartment in the building where my Aunt Tema and her family lived. After a year we moved further north where I entered a primary school that went through eighth grade. A number of my classmates belonged to the Brownies, the younger club of the Girl Scouts. I don't recall how it was that I was invited to speak about being an immigrant then. I imagine it was my best friend Jackie who invited me. I remember standing in the front of the room, facing a group of children. I can't remember what I spoke about, but I assume I described where I came from. I must have been about eleven years old.

What to tell these children now? How do I choose? My husband suggested something that had totally escaped me. "You were about the same age as these children are now. Talk about what it was like to come to America at the age of almost nine." That felt right! They could envision themselves in my shoes.

How should I begin?

Once upon a time a young girl named Fela stood on the deck of an ocean liner that crossed the Atlantic from Germany and entered the New York Harbor. She was holding her mother's hand and in the other she held her favorite doll. Her mother was wearing a black pirate patch to cover her infected eye and with her free hand was pointing to the Statue of Liberty. There was a great deal of excitement on the deck. The little girl joined the mood when she caught sight of the tall beautiful statue, a lady wearing a crown with a book in one hand, her other hand extended high into the sky holding a lighted torch. The young girl knew something important was going to happen. She was also very happy that she could finally leave the ship and get to see America, the country she had heard so much about during the years when she and her family lived in the Föhrenwald DP Camp. She was looking forward to seeing something called a television set. Her mother tried to explain that it was like the movies, but Fela did not understand how it was possible to see a movie at home. For the last eleven days she had been very afraid on the ship. A big storm had tossed the ship side to side. She felt seasick, she was sure the ship would fall in the ocean and she would drown. She was really happy to see the Lady and feel the ground beneath her.

On the lower East Side of Manhattan, in a light-filled cheerful classroom, with the walls covered with children's art work, I sit on a small chair, looking around at the diverse group of children sitting on the floor, their beautiful, eager, attentive faces looking up at me. Once more I'm reminded of the Yiddish song *Oyfn Pripetchik,* about a Rabbi in a small village in Poland teaching the Yiddish alphabet to a group of small children. How fitting it is that this school is situated on the lower East Side, traditionally a working-class immigrant neighborhood, where by the 1920s the Jewish population was the largest of the different ethnic groups that had arrived in the 19th and early 20th centuries. While the lower East Side has undergone gentrification, its neighborhoods still represent a diverse racial and ethnic population. A large number of the children have immigrant parents from different countries: Haiti, Spain, Australia, England, Greece, Peru, Puerto Rico, The Dominican Republic, and Sweden.

I begin my story: "We are now sitting not far from the harbor where I first spotted the Statue of Liberty from the ocean liner *Il Italia* which brought my family and me from Germany. There we lived in a camp set up by the Americans to give people who survived the war a place to live while they waited for visas to move to other countries. These camps were called Displaced Persons Camps and they were like small towns."

It suddenly occurred to me to ask the children if they or their families came from a different country. Many of them raised their hands and told me the countries they had come from.

I went on to explain, "I lived with my family, I went to school, rode my bicycle, and we had a big dog. My father went to work and my mother went to school to learn English. During the war, before we got to this camp, my family and I lived in many different places and this DP camp felt like home. For the first time, I felt comfortable and safe."

One of the children asked: "Were you scared of coming to America? Did you want to leave, or did you not want to leave?" I responded: "My parents very much wanted to come to America and told me excitedly about how nice it would be. But it was hard for me to leave. Change can be difficult and I couldn't actually picture what they were describing or where I would live. We also had to leave our dog behind."

"Because I did not speak English when I arrived, I was put in first grade, with classmates three years younger than me. This felt strange since I was the same age that you are now. Just think of what it would be like to be in first grade instead of in fourth grade. In the DP camp, people spoke different languages because they had come from different countries. Again, like some of you were born speaking another language, I first spoke Jewish and Russian and a little German. I first went to a Jewish school and later to a German school and learned to read, write, and memorize my multiplication tables."

A couple of children nodded and looked understanding when I said that I knew no English. "But while I spoke no English—in a short time, as if by magic—I couldn't remember ever not speaking it. I bet it is the same for some of you."

Some were sitting on chairs, others comfortably on the floor with their legs crossed. I was so impressed with their attentiveness. Only one or two of them seemed restless and needed to move around.

What else can I tell them?

"It was hard for me to get used to the strange food I was given to eat—like potato chips, pizza, peanut butter and jelly sandwiches."

The children started laughing when I said I thought pizza and chips were strange, and didn't like them.

I continued, "I was accustomed to Russian and Jewish cooking; I loved Russian cabbage soup, smoked salmon, cheese blintzes, and of course ice cream. I finally got to see what a TV looked like at my aunt's house where I went after school to watch my favorite shows, like cowboy Westerns. And I watched cartoons which I had never seen before. We would not have our own TV until a few years later and it showed only black and white pictures. I learned my first English words from watching television programs."

As I looked at the children in front of me, a few who recently had come from other countries, I searched my mind for more to tell. Less benign experiences came to mind and I found myself wearing my child therapist hat, careful not to overwhelm them with my history prior to arrival in this country. I was thinking about the many years we waited in the immigration office of the DP camp to be granted a visa to emigrate to America.

I said, "It was very hard for my parents to get a visa to come here, it took a long time. While waiting we lived in different DP camps and though it felt like home, the camps were temporary and not real homes. Today many people have no place to go and want to come to America, but aren't allowed in. Like my family, they too want to leave or escape from their countries because of wars. Leaving their homes behind, they find their way to foreign countries, unfamiliar surroundings, staying in temporary housing and camps. Yet many refugees today have much less than we had. They don't have a DP camp as safe as the one I lived in. We had organizations helping us and finally some relatives found us and brought us to America."

One of the boys interrupted me and asked me to tell about a frightening experience that happened to me. He knew about the Holocaust. Quickly, the kidnapping episode came to mind and I started to reject it and searched my memory for another example, one less disturbing. But the story stayed with me and I decided to tell it.

"This is a story my parents repeatedly told me but that I can't remember. In Poland, when I was about three years old, they used to have markets on the weekends like the Union Square Market where everybody goes and buys things. My aunt was holding my hand, and there were lots and lots of people, and there was a doll that I saw that I wanted, but my parents said they couldn't afford it. So I was very, very upset and I was crying and anyway, I ran away from my aunt, which is a terrible thing to do. You don't just let go of an adult's hand, but I did, and I guess I must have run to where the doll was. But two women saw me alone and took my hand and started to walk away with me." The boy who had asked the question said, "So what happened?"

"My parents told me how frantic they were and found a policeman who began to look for me.

The two women were just about to get into a truck with me when the policeman saw them and stopped them. My mother and father came up and started yelling at the women who claimed I was their child. I was almost kidnapped. There were not many babies during the war and so if you stole a child you could have one or even sell it.

The story has a happy ending. My parent grabbed me and hugged me. Then they scolded me for leaving my aunt's side. I was very sorry, but so happy that they had found me. They were so relieved that they bought me the doll and made me promise that I would never wander off again alone." At this point it was time to stop, and the teacher thanked me for coming as the children prepared to go.

I felt many different emotions when I finished speaking. I was deeply moved by the children's attention, openness, and curiosity. My story was of a little girl who had realized the American Dream, has become a privileged American adult who was ultimately given a safe refuge and built a permanent home. Why did I also feel saddened and spent?

The kidnapping story had turned my mind to the political climate in our country, of children and families separated at our borders, of asylum seekers refused refuge, of refugees denied permission to enter. And I thought of my own family, the years of being denied a visa because an x-ray of my father's lungs showed an old tuberculosis scar. Just as my family soldiered on seeking a safe home, so others continue to march forward across forbidding and hostile territories, serving as a testament to human resilience and the spirit of hope.

Back in April of 2013, I received a call from my friend Annie who woke from a dream about my mother and needed to share it with me:

I was walking into Sydney's apartment (Annie's sister who had died two years ago). *It was being totally transformed... at least as I viewed it at the front door. I did not go further in - new walls of reddish marble—like a mausoleum—were being constructed. It vaguely felt as if Sydney were with me. A phone rings in my head " Hello Anichka, it's Sonja." I was caught by surprise and very emotional to hear her so clearly. I stuttered "Sonya... where are you?" She responded clearly, in a few sentences... I don't remember what she said... then she said "I am not really here but don't tell Phyllis..." Then it was over. I think I was so happy to have heard your mother's voice. As I write this, I am teary... unexpectedly...*

A bit later Annie calls back:

I was just in the shower when more of the dream came to me... the marble walls had a window cut out... supposedly into a kitchen but all that could be seen was brilliant light. When your mother said "I'm not really here, don't tell Phyllis," Sydney's voice said "she's borderline..." I think now she meant that [Sonja] was on the border of leaving ... into that space behind the marble. Sydney was only accompanying me *(as she did and does) and helping me through this next stage. I hope they are together.*

The next day I wrote Annie an email:

I woke up much too early this morning and found myself thinking about the dream you had about my mother. I realized that I have been dreaming very little about my mother... not as much as I would have expected. I then had an insight about my own mourning and why I can't really articulate how I am feeling with my mother gone. I think I won't be able to fully mourn until this writing about my mother's life and my family's journey is captured in my own memoir. I started this writing project as a way of holding the memories my mother was losing, but I realize that it was also the beginning of a process of mourning her. Now that she is actually gone, it is as if I have to keep her alive until I remember her story and my own.

This brings me to your dream. When my mother told you not to tell me, I took it to mean not to tell me she was dead. So here I am taking a part of your dream as a confirmation that she can't be dead to me until I finish "her story" which is of course my story. And so, while she's still very alive for me, you, my ever- generous friend, are mourning her and sharing your startling dream.

My mother died on January 22, 2013, and I end this memoir on what would have been her ninety-sixth birthday, February 3, 2019. Coming to the end of this story has been my way of mourning her. During this mourning period, I recalled and reawakened memories, retold old stories, discovered new ones and learned history. Writing this memoir has turned out to be a gift I have given myself, reacquainting me with my family and, in the process, with myself. I've come to know my father better and understand the closeness we shared. It has been a privilege to once more mourn my father, my stepfather, my aunts and uncles in America, my grandparents and aunt who remained in Russia, and those who were lost in the Holocaust. I'm fortunate to still have Elizabeth with me telling her stories and my cousins recalling theirs. Just as it comforts me to have my mother, father, stepfather, aunts and uncles all resting in the same cemetery, I have been enlightened and moved by bringing them together in this memoir. Fela was my first name, so I am calling this book *Fela's Story: Memoir of a Displaced Family*. It has been a story of loss and of my coming home once again.

Acknowledgements

I undertook this journey with my writing group, our teacher and mentor, Jane Lazarre, and Josephine Wright, who accompanied me on her own journey. We resonated in what mattered most: how we viewed the world, our family, and friends and ourselves as women, mothers, and professionals. I was both humbled and privileged to be in the company of these two unique and extraordinary women who are now also dear friends.

    I first knew Jane Lazarre as an author whose work I deeply admired. It turned out that she was also an extraordinary and inspirational teacher, and her insight and openness always left space for me to reflect on my work. Over the time we have worked together, my admiration for her has only grown. I came to understand that her primary goal was to help me find my own voice.

    When I first heard Jo Wright read, I thought she had emerged from the womb with a notebook and pencil, describing in exquisite detail her journey through the birth canal. Jo is a psychoanalyst and a born writer whose work is evocative and poignant. She is a naturalist, and I have to thank her for bringing the Australian landscape alive before my eyes.

    Our group was also a study group, and we devoted many sessions to discussing works by women writers and to essays on the craft of writing. I am especially grateful to Jane for educating me and giving me a more profound understanding about the role of slavery and the culture of racism in our country. I thank both Jane and Jo for their unstinting enthusiasm and support for my writing.

My husband, Sheldon Bach, a psychoanalyst and author, encouraged me through every step of the way and offered very helpful suggestions. He is a gifted and beautiful writer, and he read every word I wrote more than once and, despite my skepticism, he emphatically remarked, "I like the way you said it," making it clear that he heard my voice. That meant a great deal to me and for this, and so much more, I feel love and gratitude.

I'm happily at home in a family of writers and authors, Rebecca Bach and her husband Joseph Wood, professors and authors of multiple books, Matthew Bach, an editor, and our granddaughter Jay. They were all extremely helpful and encouraging. Jay read one of the longer chapters and told me she stayed up late into the night to finish it.

I want to give a special thanks to my friends and family who knew my mother and encouraged me in writing this story.

Susan Schulson and Annie and Warren Weisberg, soulmates since first we met in college, remain an enduring presence in my life. Annie and Warren's home, not far from where my mother resided, was my second home as I flew back and forth from New York to Chicago to visit her over the five years that she lived in a senior residence. Susan and her late husband Steven always made themselves available and often visited my mother. They were my surrogate siblings, looking after her in my absence. On the weekends of my visits, Warren would break out a bottle of his fine wine and we four old friends would sit around or go out to our favorite Japanese restaurant. My soul was fed by their comfort and love. Their children, Jenny, Sarajane, Lucy, and Daniel, were my nieces and nephews. Sarajane, Matt, and their children Asher and Wyatt called my mother Mamuchka and were a part of her life. Dinners in their home were a welcome relief that cheered me on.

I'm indebted to Jenny Weisberg, who lives in New York. She and her husband Mark Landsman, both historians, took a keen interest in my memoir. Jenny, with her knowledge of Eastern European history, kept me constantly informed, researching relevant material and offering suggestions for books to read. Dinah and Alexie each invited me to their fourth-grade class on the Lower East Side to talk about my experience as an immigrant. I thank them for helping me recall what it felt like to arrive in America at the age of nine.

Lucy Schulson went to medical school in New York, and she and her brother Daniel often stayed with us and would later bring their spouses George and Dani. They frequently talked of fond memories of my mother and stepfather Chuck.

My Chicago and Detroit family of first cousins and their children and grandchildren have always been an important part of my life. Words are not sufficient to express my love and gratitude to Elizabeth Silver, who is a critical link to my past. Celebrating her 85th birthday at their lake cottage in Michigan with her children Barbara, Francine, Larry, and Jeffrey and their spouses, grandchildren, and great-great-grandchildren will remain a cherished memory. Elizabeth holds a special place in this memoir; a woman living life to the fullest, a born storyteller and comedian, fiercely devoted to family, still imbued with a capacity for optimism, laughter, and joy despite wars, suffering, and tragic losses. I feel her enduring love for me today as I did when as a child she held me in her arms.

My cousins Susan Murnick and Shar Kutko have inherited my beloved aunt Tema's goodness and warmth. Having a holiday meal at one of their homes brought me back to my aunt's house where she always made my favorite cookies. Susan, Shar and her husband Rusty would always find the time to meet me or arrange a brunch where Jan and Ryan Murnick and Kendra Kutko were there, and it comforted me to know they lived close to my mother and saw her often. It's a gift to have Lydia and Stephan Kutko and their son Dorian in New York, where they have become part of our life.

I owe a great deal to Bell Kravitz, a wonderful friend to my mother, and her late husband David, my mother's cousin. If not for David's persistence in searching and locating us in our last DP camp and helping us to come to America, my story would have a very different ending.

Delia Battin and Eugene Mahon have been ever-encouraging. Delia eagerly awaited each chapter, and her enthusiasm and thoughtful feedback warmed my heart. Steve and Carolyn Ellman's consistent friendship supported me, and their interest in history and World War II provoked stimulating discussions of our families' experiences before and after the war. I have run together with Arnie and Arlene Richards through Central Park, and also through life, for many years, and now we move more slowly, but it is still exciting. Hattie Meyers's enthusiasm for my memoir was always uplifting and her feedback invaluable. Madelon Sann Grobman and Leni Winn read early chapters and their affirming responses meant a great deal to me, as has their long and loyal friendship. I want to thank Lynne Rubin and Merrill, Jody, and Donna Lewen, longtime dear friends, for making a detour, visiting Föhrenwald, and connecting with my past.

I am deeply grateful to Ofra and David Block, who stressed the importance of keeping history alive and thus kept urging me to write my story. David and his family, like my father and paternal family, shared a similar history from Poland to the Russian labor camps, and I thank him for offering another window into the lives they led. Carol Bandini, Joyce Grossbard, Susannah Falk Lewis, Roda Neugabauer, Esther Savitz, Marge Slobetz, Rebecca Shamoon-Shanok, and Katherine Snelson are a close group of colleagues and friends who I thank for being a sustaining presence in my life since my earliest years in New York.

I want to thank Sandra Shapiro, for shedding more light on her father, David Shapiro, our dear friend and doctor in the Föhrenwald DP camp. We had lost touch in later years and, while searching for her on the internet, I discovered that she was performing at Carnegie Hall. I got in touch with her and found we were both researching information about our family's histories and that she had created a series of concerts called *In the Footsteps of my Father: A Daughter's Search for Answers*. We exchanged stories and photos about our families that helped us fill out the lives of our parents. It has been a very moving experience to come together once again.

I want to thank Graciela Abelin for listening so well to my story so many times.

I want to thank Kathy Kovacic for her inspired suggestion and use of Senya Gorodetsky's drawing of my grandparents' home in Gomel for the cover.

Finally, I want to thank my friend and publisher, Arnold Richards, who felt that this was not just another memoir, and Tamar and Larry Schwartz, who so skillfully shepherded the manuscript through publication. I don't want to omit my calico cat Kasha, who has been my loyal companion and self-contained friend for all this time.

References

Meade, R., *My Life in Middlemarch.* Broadway Books, Crown Publishing Group, a division of Radom House, NY, 2015.

Morrison, Toni., *Playing in the Dark: Whiteness and the Literary Imagination.* Vintage Books, NY, 1993.

O'Connell, M., *Why You Should Red W.G. Sebald.* The New Yorker, December 14, 2011.

Sebald, W.G., *Austerlitz,* Random House, NY 2001.

Shaw, P. , *Reading Dante,* Liveright, New York, 2014.

Waydenfeld, S. (1999), *The Ice Road: An Epic Journey from the Stalinist Labor Camps to Freedom.* Aquila Polonica (U.S.) Los Angels, CA, 2010.